Robert Frost

*The People, Places, and Stories
Behind His New England Poetry*

Robert Frost

The People, Places, and Stories
Behind His New England Poetry

Lea Newman

Foreword by Jay Parini

The New England Press, Inc.
Shelburne, Vermont

For Chick,
now that "la vita nuova" is ours

Manufactured in the United States of America
Cover watercolor by Elayne Sears
ISBN 1-881535-39-8

Early verisons of the essays accompanying "The Pasture" and "The Road Not Taken" appeared in the Fall 1999 issue of *The Mind's Eye*, published by the Massachusetts College of Liberal Arts.

05 04 03 02 01   6 5 4 3 2

For additional copies of this book or for a catalog of our other New England titles, please write:

The New England Press
P.O. Box 575
Shelburne, VT 05482

or e-mail: nep@together.net

Visit us on the Web at www.nepress.com

Library of Congress Cataloging-in-Publication Data

Newman, Lea Bertani Vozar.
   Robert Frost : the people, places, and stories behind his New England poetry / Lea Newman.-- 1st ed.
     p. cm.
   Includes bibliographical references and index.
   ISBN 1-881535-39-8
    1. Frost, Robert, 1874-1963--Knowledge--New England. 2. New England--In literature.
   3. New England--Poetry. I. Frost, Robert, 1874-1963. II. Title.

PS3511.R94 Z845 2000
811'.52--dc21
                                     00-048074

Contents

Foreword vii

Preface and Acknowledgments.. ix

Introduction xiii

1. My Butterfly 2

2. Into My Own 6

3. Reluctance 8

4. Waiting 10

5. The Tuft of Flowers 12

6. A Late Walk 16

7. Stars 18

8. The Vantage Point 20

9. Mowing 22

10. Ghost House 24

11. Rose Pogonias 28

12. October 30

13. A Prayer in Spring 32

14. My November Guest 34

15. A Time to Talk 36

16. Putting in the Seed 38

17. Going for Water 40

18. The Death of the Hired Man 42

19. Pea Brush 50

20. The Oven Bird 52

21. An Old Man's Winter Night 54

22. Hyla Brook 56

23. The Pasture 58

24. Storm Fear 60

25. Good Hours 62

26. The Wood-Pile 64

27. Mending Wall 68

28. After Apple-Picking 72

29. Birches 76

30. Home Burial 80

31. The Cow in Apple Time 86

32. The Sound of the Trees 88

33. The Exposed Nest 90

34. The Road Not Taken 94

35. "Out, Out—" 96

36. An Encounter 100

A Selective Chronology of Robert Frost's Life 102

How to Start a Frost Poetry Circle 104

Thematic Groupings of Frost's Poetry 109

Alphabetical Listing of Poems 115

Backnotes 117

Bibliography 129

Index 135

Foreword

Lea Newman, a literary scholar of considerable talent, has provided something very special here for readers and admirers of Robert Frost and his poetry. With immense common sense and a firm grip on the available scholarship, she has provided readers with an amiable walk through thirty-six of the finest poems that he wrote—poems focused on the New England landscape that, for Frost, became the terra firma of his imagination. She has gathered and sorted the biographical background to the poems, in many cases providing the kind of information (not easily available) that makes reading the poems not only more pleasurable but more stimulating as well. Her readings of such beloved poems as "The Road Not Taken," "Birches," and "Mending Wall" will open eyes. I liked the clarity of her interpretations, and her tact as well. She knows how far to go, and where the scholar must draw back. That she has included the full texts of the poems adds a great deal to the overall presentation. It's useful to turn to the poem in question, and to reread, and to meditate on the actual text. *Robert Frost: The People, Places, and Stories Behind His New England Poetry* will prove useful and entertaining as a guide to Frost's unique verbal planet. The ties that bind word and thing, poem and world, have rarely been so effectively tied.

JAY PARINI

Preface and Acknowledgments

For the three decades that I taught Robert Frost's poetry in college classrooms, he was my favorite poet for the most selfish of reasons. His poems were easy to teach. The students always enjoyed reading them, and their responses were lively and surprisingly insightful, given that most were in class not by choice but because they needed to fulfill a general education requirement. They were reluctant poetry readers at best, but they responded to Frost's poetry, and I was grateful.

My own reading of Frost's works had been haphazard. When I was in elementary school, where many of today's children read Frost for the first time, his poetry had not yet made it into the curriculum. The emphasis in the literature courses I took at Chicago Teachers College as an Education/English major was on British literature. At Wayne State University, where I entered a Master's program after fourteen years at home as a mother and corporate wife, my thesis was on the poetry of eighteenth-century England. It was not until I was a doctoral student at the University of Massachusetts at Amherst that I encountered Robert Frost in earnest in a course on Modern Poetry. What I remember most clearly about the paper I wrote on Frost's use of flower imagery was my surprise in discovering how sophisticated and talented a poet he was. Like too many casual Frost readers, I had written him off as a clever country bumpkin.

In the meantime, however, my focus was on nineteenth-century prose rather than twentieth-century poetry. And as Frost memorably put it, "knowing how way leads on to way," it would be a long time before I returned to Frost scholarship. I wrote my dissertation and my first book on Nathaniel Hawthorne's short stories, then my second on Herman Melville. I became active in the Hawthorne Society and the Melville Society, was elected president of both organizations, continued teaching at Massachusetts College of Liberal Arts (then North Adams State College)—and enjoyed the Frost classes in my Introduction to Literature courses each semester. I remember hearing a riveting talk by guest lecturer Richard Poirier at nearby Williams College on

Frost's poem "Never Again Would Birds' Song Be the Same." And I sat in on the Frost sessions at the annual Modern Language Association conference whenever they did not conflict with my Hawthorne and Melville commitments.

In 1982 the Vermont Council on the Humanities asked me to be a part of their lecture series on Vermont poets at the public library in Bennington. I agreed on condition that I could talk about Robert Frost as a Vermonter. Frost's grave in the Old First Church cemetery in Old Bennington had been the number one attraction on my standard New England sightseeing tour for out-of-state visitors since I moved to Bennington in 1968. I decided I would enjoy finding out more about him and taking a closer look at his poetry. I didn't know it then, but that research would become the starting point for this book.

It was during my first year of retirement, in 1996, that I put the book's concept into words. I was responding to a question from a local publisher about ideas I might have for a book. I told her a guide to Frost's New England poetry, written for the general public, was needed, but I was quick to add that I could not possibly handle it. I was getting ready for a month-long research trip tracing Hawthorne and Melville's travels in Italy. Not until 1998 did the idea resurface, and finally I found my way clear to taking on the project.

Fortunately an impressive number of Frost scholars had laid the groundwork for my study. This book could not have been written without the biographies, memoirs, collections of letters, critical studies, and interpretative essays that preceded it. The backnotes and the bibliography testify to my immense debt. Much has been said about Lawrance Thompson turning Frost into a monster in his biographical accounts, but all Frost scholarship has benefited from Thompson's meticulous record of the details of Frost's life, mine more than most. I found Jay Parini's 1999 biography especially helpful for its balanced approach and perceptive insights, and for the new primary material it provided. Jeffrey Cramer's book, *Robert Frost Among His Poems*, saved me an enormous amount of work by bringing together the biographical contexts and associations for each poem. It is an essential tool, impeccably researched, that belongs in every Frost scholar's library.

I am grateful to Massachusetts College of Liberal Arts for the use of their library resources and the support they have made available to me.

The Bennington Free Library has facilitated essential inter-library loans, and Jill Hays, book collector and poet in her own right, has generously allowed me free access to her Frost collection. Carole Thompson, founder of The Friends of Robert Frost, has led me to the wealth of information available on the internet and alerted me to issues that were crucial in my continuing to write this book. The one person who was instrumental in getting me started is Tordis Isselhardt, proprietor of "Images from the Past," whose interest sparked mine and whose positive response propelled me into turning my idea into a plan and ultimately into this book. My long-time mentor, Everett Emerson, who was my dissertation director and editor of my books on Hawthorne and Melville, came through once again with invaluable advice. My publisher Al Rosa and my editor Mark Wanner at New England Press genially cooperated with changes I initiated after my original proposal and have made the "business" of publishing a book as painless and pleasant a process as writers ordinarily find only in their dreams. Mark Wanner's editing has been perceptive and invariably "on target," help-ing me to write a clearer and more focused book than I could have without his feedback and guidance.

A different but equally essential kind of help has come from the members of my writing group, who for the past two years have pa-tiently listened to my problems, carefully critiqued many of the es-says in the book, prodded me when I faltered, and applauded when I persevered. My heartfelt thanks go to Sue Beal, Ellen Perry Berke-ley, Nancy Boardman, Adriana Millenaar Brown, Anna Chapman, Anne Mausolff, and Molly Stone. Three other writers, Tara Amuso, Sergine Dixon, and Lyle Glazier, have also helped with good advice and generous praise.

My two oldest and closest Vermont friends, Carol Hewitt and Celine Hoffman, have leant me moral support and encouragement from the beginning, as have Virginia Davis and Ann Vliet, former colleagues who were good enough to read early versions of some of my "stories to go with the poems." The network of friends I have made in Bennington since my retirement has become an important part of the new pattern of my life—Teresa King, Mary Kirkpatrick, Dorothy Polatsek, and the rest of the South Street Café Friday lunch regulars have helped by honoring my "writing days" and monitoring my progress on the "Frost book."

A lifetime of gratitude goes to my large and loving family. Throughout this and every other endeavor I have attempted, I have had their unconditional support and understanding. I am grateful to all of them: to Cam and Hinda and my Vozar grandchildren, Elaine, Andrea, and Steve in Michigan; to Donna and Don and the Olendorf clan, also in Michigan: Annie and Garry and their son Jacob; Stony and Kristy and their son Caleb; and Sara and Bob and their son Stanley; to Linda and Roger and my "Sweet" grandson, Adam, in New Mexico; to Mary and Paul and my twin grandchildren in Colorado, Monroe and Mattie Ivy; and to Bob, my Vermonter who also chooses to live in Colorado. To my Newman family as well: to Monica in Georgia; and to Meredith, Henry, and the Maroni boys, Sean and Evan, in Virginia.

My largest debt of gratitude goes to my husband "Chick" Newman. He has lived with Robert Frost since 1998 and has magnanimously accepted this intruder into our daily lives. He agreed to serve as my trial reader, a task he was perfectly qualified to perform. As a highly literate but non-literary person, a former engineer with the Bell system and a flight pilot and instructor, he was an ideal reader. I doubt if "Chick" has ever voluntarily read a poem in his entire life. If he could respond to the poems I chose to include and if he could understand the background essays that accompanied them, I knew I had a good chance of reaching my audience. The experiment worked remarkably well. His input was invaluable, and we have come to know each other better than we ever have before in the twenty-four years since we were married. He managed to turn his competitor into an ally.

The truth is there has been another man in my life. My affair with Robert Frost and his poetry has been consuming, often overwhelming, always exhilarating, and utterly satisfying. My hope is that this book will communicate the joy I experienced to others. I wrote my first two books for scholars and academics. This one draws on my research skills and critical expertise to serve my love of teaching. If I have succeeded, I will have transformed the facts I unearthed about this poet, his life, and his work into a guide for newcomers to Frost's poetry, the same kind of readers who responded to Frost in my introductory literature classes.

Introduction

"I want to be a poet for all sorts and kinds," Robert Frost said. In keeping with Frost's wish, the goal of this book is to give the general public convenient access to the poems for which Frost is best known, those steeped in the landscape and lore of New England. To help all sorts and kinds of people increase their understanding and appreciation of Frost's poetry, a story/essay accompanies each poem, providing the reader with the details of the place, person, incident, or emotion that inspired it.

The narrative/commentaries paired with the poems draw primarily on Frost's accounts of his life and his writing. His own words provide insights into where and when he wrote each poem, the circumstances reflected in it, and sometimes what his intentions were. For the poems whose meanings have proved controversial, some of the more striking interpretations by others are also included. Each essay brings together relevant facts and anecdotes drawn from the wealth of biographies, memoirs, interviews, and critical commentaries Frost's work has generated.

The poems are arranged chronologically according to when they were written, but not necessarily when they were published because Frost often postponed publishing his poems for years. Occasionally the composition date of a poem remains elusive, but enough data is available to establish an informed "most likely" chronology. Frost wrote the thirty-six poems reprinted in this anthology between 1892 and 1916. They were chosen from Frost's first three books of poetry: *A Boy's Will* published in 1913, *North of Boston* published in 1914, and *Mountain Interval* published in 1916. The poetry is reprinted here as it appears in these three collections.

Beginning with a significant but less-than-perfect poem he wrote as an eighteen-year-old freshman at Dartmouth, the collection builds to such celebrated masterpieces as "Mending Wall" and "After Apple Picking," written twenty years later when he was living in England, intensely homesick for the New England he had left behind. Reading the poems in the order that Frost wrote them shows how his unique voice and style developed, but glimmers of his intuitive genius come through in all the poems, whether he was writing them at eighteen or forty-two.

Frost once chastised his friend Sidney Cox for interpreting his poems biographically. He said: "I have written to keep the over curious out of the secret places of my mind . . . My objection to your larger book about me was that it came thrusting in where I did not want you." In an earlier letter to Cox, he wrote: "You must not disillusion your admirers with the tale of your sources and processes. This is the gospel according to me." In typical Frost fashion, he contradicted himself immediately, adding: "Not that I bother much to live up to it." Indeed he himself told Cox that every one of his poems is based on an actual experience.

The background essays in this book do precisely what Frost told Cox not to do. They are tales about sources and processes. Some of them do attempt to probe the secret places of Frost's mind. Like Cox's book, they may be guilty of thrusting in where Frost does not want us. But their intent is to illuminate the poetry. When Frost admitted to his poems being "autobiographical," he gave implicit permission to his admirers to follow his lead.

During the many years I spent teaching Robert Frost's poetry to college students in introductory literature courses, I was able to hone my instincts to recognize what the lay reader responds to in his poetry. He has a popular appeal second to none, but few of my students went on to enjoy his poetry on their own. This book is designed to get newcomers to poetry interested in reading more Frost poems. Its format invites browsing. The book can be opened at random to any poem and its accompanying "story," ready to provide instant access to a rich array of background details that help the reader more fully experience the poem.

The backnotes at the end of the book contain a listing of the sources where the data and quotations originated. The notes are organized by paragraph number under the title of each poem. The bibliography gives the full title and publication information for the works cited in the backnotes. The "Selective Chronology of Robert Frost's Life" is included to give readers a time frame for the wealth of details covered in the background essays.

The section titled "How to Start A Frost Poetry Circle" was frankly an after-thought. From the beginning I hoped my book would lead readers to enjoy the poetry. As I wrote it, I realized that a natural next step would be to share the pleasure with others. That is what motivates my teaching of literature. The essays in the book take the place of the teacher as the source of information about the poem. The poetry circle appendix extends the book's role as teacher by offering suggestions on how a small group of readers can implement discussions for themselves. The list of "thematic groupings" can also be used by individual readers to explore alternative approaches to the poetry, thereby enriching its possibilities.

In featuring poems that focus on Frost's sense of place, this collection follows Frost's own literary theories. He proclaimed that "literature begins with geography." Once again, however, he contradicted himself. In a piece of advice he gave to his students, he said: "There ought to be in everything you write some sign that you come from almost anywhere." In his poems Robert Frost was able to bridge that contradiction between "geography," a place you can locate on a map, and "anywhere," a concept held in the mind. He was astutely aware of what he was doing. "I talk about the whole world in terms of New England," he said. His claim is verified in demographic terms by the more than 20,000 copies of his collected poems sold each year all over the United States and abroad. Frost could and did reconcile the specific with the universal, a feat proclaimed by no less an authority than Coleridge as the defining hallmark of true poetry.

In a line from a poem not included in this collection, Frost tells us: "All the fun's in how you say a thing." All the fun can also be in how you read a Frost poem. This is a new kind of Frost anthology, intended ultimately to inspire you to enjoy the fun in Frost's way of saying things.

Robert Frost

The People, Places, and Stories
Behind His New England Poetry

1

My Butterfly

In the fall of 1892, on one of his many long and solitary walks in the countryside around Hanover, New Hampshire, Robert Frost came across a fragile butterfly wing among the leaves that covered the ground. He was a young man of eighteen, a freshman at Dartmouth College, with a secret yearning to be a poet—and he responded to the image of vulnerability and death he found in the woods with a poem.

Two years later it was published for pay in the New York magazine *The Independent,* his first success in the world of professional poetry. Between his initial encounter with the butterfly wing and the poem's publication on November 8, 1894, however, Frost's circumstances had changed drastically. Before the first term at Dartmouth was over, he had grown impatient with the stultifying routine of class schedules and assignments and had decided he could educate himself better on his own. By late winter of 1894, he was a twenty-year-old college drop-out teaching in a district school in Salem, New Hampshire. He lived with his mother and sister in a crowded apartment on Tremont Street near the railroad track in Lawrence, Massachusetts—and wrote poetry surreptitiously every chance he could get.

One Sunday evening he locked himself in the kitchen, the one room in the apartment with heat, to work on his poetry. His sister Jeanie wanted to be let in, but he ignored her banging and kicking on the door, intent only on perfecting the poem in front of him. In spite of the less than serene circumstances, Frost later remembered feeling for the first time that something extraordinary was happening to him: "It was like cutting along a nerve." "The Butterfly," he said, was his "first real poem."

Many years later, when he was advising a class of would-be writers to "get the *stuff* of life into the technique of your writing," he remembered this feeling. "I recall distinctly," he told them, "the joy with which I had the first satisfaction of getting an expression adequate for my thought. I was so delighted that I had to cry. It was the second stanza of the little poem on the Butterfly, written in my eighteenth year."

He included it in a collection of five poems he called "Twilight" that a job-printer published for him in a private edition of two copies. In an extravagant gesture that all but depleted his meager funds, he had the slender volumes leather-bound and printed on antique paper, one for himself and the other for the girl he wanted to marry, Elinor White. Nineteen years later, when Frost's first book of poetry was published in London, "My Butterfly" was the only poem from the "Twilight" group he chose to include. It remains the earliest poem to appear in the definitive collection of his poetry.

It is, however, the least Frost-like of his collected poems, lacking the distinctively American rhythms and diction that have become his trademarks. In retrospect, Frost recognized its shortcomings. "When I first began to write poetry," he said, "I was writing largely, though not exclusively, after the pattern of the past. For every poet begins that way—following some pattern, or group of patterns. It is only when he has outgrown the pattern and sees clearly for himself his own way that he has really started to become. You may go back to all those early poems of mine . . . You will find me there using the traditional cliches. . . . in my very first poem, 'My Butterfly,' I was even guilty of 'theeing' and 'thouing,' a crime I have not committed since." He went on to explain: "The young poet is prone to echo all the pleasant sounds he has heard in his scattered reading. He is apt to look on the musical value of the lines, the metrical perfection, as all that matters. He has not listened for the voice within his mind, speaking the lines and giving them the value of sound."

When he included "My Butterfly" in his first *Collected Poems*, he left the poem as first printed—"for sentiment, perhaps," he said. Whatever his reasoning, he chose not to totally disown his first "real poem," giving his readers an opportunity to appreciate the difference between his earliest poetic attempts and his subsequent mastery of a unique New England voice.

My Butterfly

Thine emulous fond flowers are dead, too,
And the daft sun-assaulter, he
That frighted thee so oft, is fled or dead:
Save only me
(Nor is it sad to thee!)
Save only me
There is none left to mourn thee in the fields.

The gray grass is not dappled with the snow;
Its two banks have not shut upon the river;
But it is long ago—
It seems forever—
Since first I saw thee glance,
With all the dazzling other ones,
In airy dalliance,
Precipitate in love,
Tossed, tangled, whirled and whirled above,
Like a limp rose-wreath in a fairy dance.

When that was, the soft mist
Of my regret hung not on all the land,
And I was glad for thee,
And glad for me, I wist.

Thou didst not know, who tottered, wandering on high,
That fate had made thee for the pleasure of the wind,
With those great careless wings,
Nor yet did I.
And there were other things:
It seemed God let thee flutter from his gentle clasp:
Then fearful he had let thee win
Too far beyond him to be gathered in,

Snatched thee, o'er eager, with ungentle grasp.
Ah! I remember me
How once conspiracy was rife
Against my life—
The languor of it and the dreaming fond;
Surging, the grasses dizzied me of thought,
The breeze three odors brought,
And a gem-flower waved in a wand!

Then when I was distraught
And could not speak,
Sidelong, full on my cheek,
What should that reckless zephyr fling
But the wild touch of thy dye-dusty wing!

I found that wing broken to-day!
For thou art dead, I said,
And the strange birds say.
I found it with the withered leaves
Under the eaves.

2

Into My Own

When Robert Frost taught in District School Number Nine in South Salem, New Hampshire, he walked through the woods for almost four miles from his mother's home in Lawrence, Massachusetts. On his daily walks during the 1894 spring term, he kept hoping "to feel really lost in the woods," but he "never realized that hope" because he would invariably come across a familiar path or landmark and know exactly where he was. At school, while his students worked on assignments at their desks, he often sat by the window and looked out into the woods. With his paper on the sill, he put down in words what he imagined it would be like to lose himself in the "dark trees" he could see on the horizon. The emotion became the impetus for the first verse of "Into My Own," but the lines he scribbled down in that schoolroom did not become a full-fledged poem until 1901. By then he had given up schoolteaching for farming and was writing poetry late into the night after his farm chores were completed and everyone else had gone to bed.

In a letter to a close friend, he said he "went away from people (and college)" in this poem, referring to two pivotal events in his life in the years immediately preceding his semester at the Salem district school: leaving Dartmouth College before he had finished his first semester there and running away from home to the Dismal Swamp in Virginia after Elinor appeared to reject him. The second verse echoes his attempt to "steal away" into the "vastness" of the wooded swamp in Virginia where, unlike the woods in Salem, he could—and did—get lost.

Similarly, the third verse's wistful hope that those he left behind might come after him corresponds with his estrangement from Elinor. That connection is reinforced by the phrase "the edge of doom" that comes from Shakespeare's sonnet 116 about the enduring nature of love.

The closing couplet has elicited the broadest range of responses. Some readers see it as the bravado of a boasting adolescent, others as the stubborn resistance to change at the heart of all of Frost's poetry. Frost's own interpretation favors the second. He said the two lines were "really about loyalty" and declared he never accepted "the

Emersonian idea of being pleased with your own inconsistency." At a poetry reading in 1962, more than six decades after he had completed the poem, he reiterated his position by adding, after an energetic reading of the last two lines: "That, again, is a certainty."

Frost also said this poem was about his "desire for the wilderness." One of the strongest recurring images in his poetry is a stand of dark woods that invites him to enter and lose himself. Archibald MacLeish, himself a poet from New England, believes "the longing for the dark" was in Frost, but "the image that contains that longing is a New England image." He points to this poem as a prime example of how Frost uses "a characteristic New England scene: that view across open pasture toward the line of trees that ends the open everywhere in Massachusetts or New Hampshire or Vermont." He comes to the startling conclusion that "the man at the pasture's edge on one side, the trees against the sky at the other, compose the poem between them," in effect making the New England landscape Frost's co-writer.

Into My Own

One of my wishes is that those dark trees,
So old and firm they scarcely show the breeze,
Were not, as 'twere, the merest mask of gloom,
But stretched away unto the edge of doom.

I should not be withheld but that some day
Into their vastness I should steal away,
Fearless of ever finding open land,
Or highway where the slow wheel pours the sand.

I do not see why I should e'er turn back,
Or those should not set forth upon my track
To overtake me, who should miss me here
And long to know if still I held them dear.

They would not find me changed from him they knew—
Only more sure of all I thought was true.

3

Reluctance

Robert Frost was suffering from a broken heart when he wrote "Reluctance." He believed the woman he loved no longer loved him. In his mind, Elinor White had rejected him when she refused to let him in after he showed up unexpectedly at her door at St. Lawrence University. He had arrived with a gift, a book of his poems printed especially for her, and he could not accept her explanation that she was only following campus rules.

Desperate with the suspicion that Elinor was interested in someone else, he decided to run away and lose himself in the wilderness of the Dismal Swamp in Virginia. Frost's melodramatic plan turned into a month-long series of mundane misadventures, and his disappearance seemed to have had little effect on Elinor.

The anguish he felt was sufficiently real, however, to compel him to set it down in verse in late fall 1894 after his return to Lawrence. The first stanza is about leaving home and then returning to find things "ended." The next two stanzas enlist nature as a mirror to his sense of loss. In a public reading of this poem, Frost said, "Even a season—that pain of the end of summer—is in it for me." The poem's last line reaffirms this linkage of "love" and "season."

A key to the change that takes place during the course of the poem—from sadness and resignation to hope and determination—is provided in a letter dated about the same time he wrote the poem. In it, he declares himself no longer "morbid now"; he had returned from the Dismal Swamp to find his first poem, "My Butterfly," in print, and he tells his publisher he will be submitting more poems. Whether it be his aspiration to write poetry or to win Elinor's love, Frost refuses to accept defeat. He thought sticking to one's goals, whatever the odds, was being loyal to oneself. In a talk in 1948 titled "Speaking of Loyalty," he said he had "written a great deal about it; once away back when I was very young in a stanza I'll venture to say to you." What he read was the last verse of "Reluctance."

Reluctance

Out through the fields and the woods
 And over the walls I have wended;
I have climbed the hills of view
 And looked at the world, and descended;
I have come by the highway home,
 And lo, it is ended.

The leaves are all dead on the ground,
 Save those that the oak is keeping
To ravel them one by one
 And let them go scraping and creeping
Out over the crusted snow,
 When others are sleeping.

And the dead leaves lie huddled and still,
 No longer blown hither and thither;
The last lone aster is gone;
 The flowers of the witch-hazel wither;
The heart is still aching to seek,
 But the feet question 'Whither?'

Ah, when to the heart of man
 Was it ever less than a treason
To go with the drift of things,
 To yield with a grace to reason,
And bow and accept the end
 Of a love or a season?

4

Waiting

Few ever heard Robert Frost read this poem, because he thought it too "personal" for public recitations. He remembered having written it before 1895, the year that he and Elinor were married, but he wasn't sure if it was in Lawrence, Massachusetts, or Salem, New Hampshire. Frost lived in both places during the years he and Elinor were separated while she attended classes at St. Lawrence University. She is the "one absent" in the next to the last line of the poem.

During those years Frost worked at a series of odd jobs, but primarily he spent his time waiting—waiting to be able to devote himself to writing poetry and waiting for Elinor to agree to marry him. In "Waiting" he succeeds in doing the first by writing about the second.

It is, as Frost himself called it, a "gentle" poem. The setting is a New England hayfield where both the time of year and the time of day are times of waiting: the uniform haystacks waiting to be harvested before winter's arrival and the moon's rising light waiting for the sun's rays to disappear. The speaker is alone except for the field's natural inhabitants: hawks, bats, a swallow, and a cricket in the haycock, all of which he captures with detailed imagery. He dreams "on" these things in nature, he says, and on two things more: the book he has brought with him and the loved one he misses for whom he wrote these lines.

The book he holds is Francis Palgrave's *Golden Treasury*, an anthology of "all the best original Lyrical pieces and Songs" in the English language. Frost bought it when he was at Dartmouth College, and he cherished it all his life, reading it to his children and assigning it to his students.

The tone of the poem best fits the time frame of spring 1895, when Elinor was completing her final semester at St. Lawrence and their engagement had reached a less turbulent phase. The autumnal setting would then have been a remembrance of the past three New England falls he had endured away from her. Whatever the specific date of composition, "Waiting" must have helped in Frost's campaign to overcome Elinor's doubts. They married in December 1895, but, unfortunately, their courtship foreshadowed a sometimes combative marriage.

Waiting

AFIELD AT DUSK

What things for dream there are when spectre-like,
Moving among tall haycocks lightly piled,
I enter alone upon the stubble field,
From which the laborers' voices late have died,
And in the antiphony of afterglow
And rising full moon, sit me down
Upon the full moon's side of the first haycock
And lose myself amid so many alike.

I dream upon the opposing lights of the hour,
Preventing shadow until the moon prevail;
I dream upon the night-hawks peopling heaven,
Each circling each with vague unearthly cry,
Or plunging headlong with fierce twang afar;
And on the bat's mute antics, who would seem
Dimly to have made out my secret place,
Only to lose it when he pirouettes,
And seek it endlesly with purblind haste;
On the last swallow's sweep; and on the rasp
In the abyss of odor and rustle at my back,
That, silenced by my advent, finds once more,
After an interval, his instrument,
And tries once—twice—and thrice if I be there;
And on the worn book of old-golden song
I brought not here to read, it seems, but hold
And freshen in this air of withering sweetness;
But on the memory of one absent most,
For whom these lines when they shall greet her eye.

5

The Tuft of Flowers

During his summer vacation in 1891, between his junior and senior year of high school, Robert Frost worked on the "haying" crew on John Dinsmore's farm near Salem, New Hampshire. Back then the grass was "mowed by hand . . . in the dew of the morning." Then it was his job "to toss the grass, open it up, let the sun at it." One day, as he "turned" the grass after the mower, he saw a single blossoming plant still standing tall, spared from the mower's scythe that had leveled everything else around it.

The summer job lasted only three weeks, but the image was indelibly fixed in Frost's consciousness, and it became the inspiration for "The Tuft of Flowers." Exactly when he wrote it is uncertain, although Frost remembered it as "one of the earliest I ever wrote . . . back in the nineties." When he entered Harvard as a special student in 1897, he had a draft of it ready to use as a theme assignment in his English composition class. The piece did not impress the instructor, who wanted the students to limit themselves to rhetorical "exercises," and Frost was outraged when he received a final grade of "B" in the course.

The poem waited another nine years before it was published, and then not until after Frost used it to get a teaching position at Pinkerton Academy. In the same way, he said, that "little Tommy Tucker sang for his supper," he was asked to present a poem at the Congregationalist Men's League banquet to introduce himself to the leaders of the church who ran the school. It was actually the minister, Charles Merriam, who did the "singing," because Frost had never publicly read his poetry and was "too timid to read it" himself. According to Frost's account, "it made a hit, and again my poetry saved me." He got the teaching position he badly needed, and getting the poem printed in the March 9, 1906, edition of the local newspaper, *The Derry Enterprise*, was almost anticlimactic.

Ordinarily, Frost disliked identifying themes in his poetry, but on several occasions he said the subject of this poem was "togetherness." "I was thinking both ways: together and alone," he explained. He had gone "away from people"—referring to his solitary life as a farmer, but in "A Tuft of Flowers" he "came back to them actually as well as verbally." "Actually" refers to the instrumental role the poem played in getting him a teaching appointment where he would be interacting with others. By "verbally" he means within the poem itself when he countermands the "alone" in line 8 with the "together" in line 39, emphasizing the change by repeating the line: "Whether they work together or apart."

He linked this poem with others he had written on the "same subject"—his position "between socialism and individualism"—but he emphasized that "the social part of it is secondary." He wanted his readers to understand that the mower saved the flowers because he liked them, not for any self-conscious reason of doing it for the sake of others. "The heart of the whole thing" he said, is "in the line: 'from sheer morning gladness at the brim.'" He believed "That's where the poetry transcends sociology."

It was always the poetry, not the message, that was important to Frost. He claimed this poem contains a definition of poetry. He drew a parallel between the mower and the poet in that the poet writes his poem and leaves it to flourish for others. But, he warned, "exhibitionism" should not be involved; this poem was "against the idea that you write poetry just to show yourself off." The motivating force is the spontaneous pleasure created by a sight or a sound or an experience. The overflowing joy felt by the speaker in response to the flower is the same emotion that prompts the poet to write poetry.

In a letter to his friend Louis Untermeyer, Frost wrote: "A poem is never a put-up job . . . It begins as a lump in the throat . . . It is never a thought to begin with." In his essay "The Figure a Poem Makes," Frost develops this concept further. A poem, he writes, "begins in delight and ends in wisdom." It "must be a revelation . . . as much for the poet as for the reader." "A Tuft of Flowers" meets Frost's criteria on all counts. Not surprisingly, it earned its creator's approval. It was a poem, Frost said, "I always considered one of my best."

The Tuft of Flowers

I went to turn the grass once after one
Who mowed it in the dew before the sun.

The dew was gone that made his blade so keen
Before I came to view the levelled scene.

I looked for him behind an isle of trees;
I listened for his whetstone on the breeze.

But he had gone his way, the grass all mown,
And I must, as he had been,—alone,

'As all must be,' I said within my heart,
'Whether they work together or apart.'

But as I said it, swift there passed me by
On noiseless wing a 'wildered butterfly,

Seeking with memories grown dim o'er night
Some resting flower of yesterday's delight.

And once I marked his flight go round and round,
As where some flower lay withering on the ground.

And then he flew as far as eye could see,
And then on tremulous wing came back to me.

I thought of questions that have no reply,
And would have turned to toss the grass to dry;

But he turned first, and led my eye to look
At a tall tuft of flowers beside a brook,

A leaping tongue of bloom the scythe had spared
Beside a reedy brook the scythe had bared.

I left my place to know them by their name,
Finding them butterfly weed when I came.

The mower in the dew had loved them thus,
By leaving them to flourish, not for us,

Nor yet to draw one thought of ours to him,
But from sheer morning gladness at the brim.

The butterfly and I had lit upon,
Nevertheless, a message from the dawn,

That made me hear the wakening birds around,
And hear his long scythe whispering to the ground,

And feel a spirit kindred to my own;
So that henceforth I worked no more alone;

But glad with him, I worked as with his aid,
And weary, sought at noon with him the shade;

And dreaming, as it were, held brotherly speech
With one whose thought I had not hoped to reach.

'Men work together,' I told him from the heart,
'Whether they work together or apart.'

6

A Late Walk

By 1897, the year that Robert Frost said he wrote this poem, he had lived through twelve autumns in New England, having moved there in 1885 as a boy of eleven. "A Late Walk" captures the regret Frost felt each year with the passing of summer. He included it in his first book, *A Boy's Will*, where Frost arranged the poems to fit into the theme of a boy's growing up. This poem was accompanied by the commentary: "He courts the autumnal mood."

Frost was writing from first hand experience in this poem—the mowed field, the garden, the last leaf on a bare tree, and the final flower of the season are all personal memories. He had created "the headless aftermath" himself when he was part of a haying crew, first on Loren Bailey's farm in Salem, New Hampshire, in 1889 when he was fifteen, and two years later on John Dinsmore's farm at Cobbett's Pond in the same area.

The year before he wrote the poem, a garden had been one of the features he and his new wife had especially enjoyed at the cottage they rented in Allenstown, New Hampshire. Their friend Carl Burell planted the garden—and the flowers around the cottage—before they arrived. He arranged the rental for them, providing an idyllic setting for their belated honeymoon vacation that summer of 1896.

Under the circumstances, it's not surprising that this was originally written as a love poem for Elinor, who is clearly the "you" in the last stanza. Frost often went out for solitary walks that summer, because Elinor's advanced pregnancy made it difficult for her to accompany him, and he invariably returned with a gift of flowers. Another poem, "Flower Gathering," written while they were living there, focuses on the wildflowers he brought back for her. "A Late Walk" is a retrospective look at the same setting in late summer. The faded aster he gives her comes "not far from my going forth," that is, from the flowers that had bloomed all summer long around the cottage they shared—the cottage that, with the advent of autumn, they would soon be leaving.

A Late Walk

When I go up through the mowing field,
  The headless aftermath,
Smooth-laid like thatch with the heavy dew,
  Half closes the garden path.

And when I come to the garden ground,
  The whir of sober birds
Up from the tangle of withered weeds
  Is sadder than any words.

A tree beside the wall stands bare,
  But a leaf that lingered brown,
Disturbed, I doubt not, by my thought,
  Comes softly rattling down.

I end not far from my going forth
  By picking the faded blue
Of the last remaining aster flower
  To carry again to you.

7

Stars

One of the most painful events in Robert Frost's life shaped this poem, changing it from a nature poem describing a winter scene to a bitter observation on an uncaring and inscrutable universe. Between the time he started writing it in 1898 or 1899 and the time he completed it in 1900 Frost lost his first-born son, Elliott, to "cholera infantum." To add to Frost's trauma, he felt responsible for the three-year-old boy's death. A homeopath recommended by Frost's mother had prescribed some pills, but when Elliott's condition worsened, the Frosts called in their own medical doctor. He told them: "It's too late now for me to do anything. The child will be dead before morning." Elliot died that night, July 8, 1900.

Frost thought his son's death was punishment for having delayed calling the doctor. Elinor, who had fallen into a deep depression, berated Frost for such a self-centered belief, pointing out that she and Elliott were brutally hurt too. Besides, she said, she didn't believe there was a God to assign the punishment. Frost never totally embraced his wife's atheism, but in this poem, his grief and guilt drove him to express the possibility that, as he said in the commentary that originally accompanied it: "There is no oversight of human affairs." The shift in outlook occurs in the third verse, where the symbolic stars of the second verse that held a "keenness for our fate" are now viewed as being capable of "neither love nor hate."

Two images dominate this poem—stars and snow. It opens with a typical New England winter landscape, cold and white. The night sky is filled with stars, the earth below marked by giant mounds of wind-shaped snow, "tall as trees." The scene is made emblematic of death, when the reader is reminded that "Our faltering steps" will lead us to the final "place of rest"—the "white rest" that is a snow covered grave. The death motif is carried to the close of the poem in the marble statue of Minerva, the Roman goddess of wisdom, whose "snow-white" eyes are blind to the injustices in the world. She is as cold, white, and lifeless as the stars over the wintry scene—and just as uncaring.

Stars

How countlessly they congregate
  O'er our tumultuous snow,
Which flows in shapes as tall as trees
  When wintry winds do blow! —

As if with keenness for our fate,
  Our faltering few steps on
To white rest, and a place of rest
  Invisible at dawn, —

And yet with neither love nor hate,
  Those stars like some snow-white
Minerva's snow-white marble eyes
  Without the gift of sight.

8

The Vantage Point

"The Vantage Point" sets a vintage New England scene: cows grazing in a pasture, a grove of trees across one horizon, a village with its white frame houses and adjoining cemetery across another. In the foreground, a solitary figure stretches out on a gently sloping hillside dotted with pale-blue wildflowers.

The only thing more Yankee in this poem than the setting is the attitude of the speaker. His idea of seeking out mankind is to come out of the woods long enough to spend one morning gazing at far-away houses and graves from a spot where he remains hidden from view. In what is almost a caricature of the isolated New Englander, he opts for nature over society. He rejects intercourse with "mankind" in favor of the earth, the bluets, and an ant colony.

Frost's original title for this poem, "Choice of Society," emphasizes the preference for the natural world over the social entanglements of the town. When he wrote it in 1900, he, his wife, and young daughter Lesley had just moved from Methuen, just outside the mill town of Lawrence, Massachusetts, to a poultry farm near Derry, New Hampshire. They soon found themselves enjoying the change to country living. Frost had little contact with the people in the village—his interests focused instead on the farm and his family.

Much like the speaker in the poem who can spend the day reclining on a hillside enjoying nature's company, Frost was free from the constraints of an employer's demands. Nostalgia colors his many remembrances of the Derry farm. It was a place, he emphasized repeatedly, where he had the "time and seclusion" he needed to observe and to write. He credited the Derry landscape, a view of which he gives us in this poem, with being "the terrain of my poetry" and the Derry years as being at "the core of all my writing."

Frost's happy acceptance of the isolation on the farm is reflected in "The Vantage Point." Paradoxically, out of these years apart from the world came the heart of the poetry that would open up a dialogue between Frost and his readers all over the world.

The Vantage Point

If tired of trees I seek again mankind,
  Well I know where to hie me—in the dawn,
  To a slope where the cattle keep the lawn.
There amid lolling juniper reclined,
Myself unseen, I see in white defined
  Far off the homes of men, and farther still,
  The graves of men on an opposing hill,
Living or dead, whichever are to mind.
And if by noon I have too much of these,
  I have but to turn on my arm, and lo,
  The sun-burned hillside sets my face aglow,
My breathing shakes the bluet like a breeze,
  I smell the earth, I smell the bruisèd plant,
  I look into the crater of the ant.

9

Mowing

Robert Frost was fifteen years old when he learned to use a scythe on Loren Bailey's farm in Salem, New Hampshire. He and his mother and sister were living in rooms they rented from the Baileys, and he was asked to help with the haying. His first attempts at mowing were clumsy, the blade bending the grass down instead of cutting it. Mr. Bailey taught him to position the blade flat to the ground and to steady his stance and backswing.

In 1900, when Frost wrote this poem, he was haying for himself on the Derry farm and had become proficient enough to take pleasure in the experience. He devoted his days to the work on the farm but stayed up at night to work on his poetry. He found the chores imposed on him as a full-time farmer during the day could become the raw material for the poems he wrote as a part-time poet at night.

In "Mowing," Frost transforms the making of hay into the making of poetry. Not only does Frost convey the common sounds and sights on his New Hampshire farm—the "whispering" scythe, the hot sun, "pale orchises," and "a bright green snake"—but he uses them to express what he was just beginning to realize: that the *facts* of everyday existence could also be the stuff of *dreams*. He often singled out line 13 ("The fact is the sweetest dream that labor knows") as the "one line" that could explain his personal "philosophy of art." It was, he said, his "definition of poetry": "Doting on things, gloating on things, just dwelling on things. Not getting up things, not exaggerating things, not whooping things up, but just gloating." He attributed his success as a poet to having had "a lot to do" with this habit of anchoring his poetry in things. He went so far as to admit: "In Mowing, for instance, I come so near what I long to get that I almost despair of coming nearer."

This poem marks another significant breakthrough in Frost's development as a poet. It is the first time he uses his informal colloquial voice to create what he calls "talk song," a way of combining the meter and form of poetry with the diction and rhythm of human speech. Frost thought "Mowing" was the best poem in his first book. It was a piece of writing about which he could proudly proclaim: "Yes, now that's perfectly clear, straight goods—mine."

Mowing

There was never a sound beside the wood but one,
And that was my long scythe whispering to the ground.
What was it it whispered? I knew not well myself;
Perhaps it was something about the heat of the sun,
Something, perhaps, about the lack of sound —
And that was why it whispered and did not speak.
It was no dream of the gift of idle hours,
Or easy gold at the hand of fay or elf;
Anything more than the truth would have seemed too weak
To the earnest love that laid the swale in rows,
Not without feeble-pointed spikes of flowers
(Pale orchises), and scared a bright green snake.
The fact is the sweetest dream that labor knows.
My long scythe whispered and left the hay to make.

10

Ghost House

Robert Frost once described his years on the Derry farm as "a time when my eyes and ears were open, very open." This was certainly true when he wrote this poem in 1901. He had been on the farm a little over a year, and "Ghost House" confirms that he had all his powers of observation in top working order—and an active literary imagination as well.

The image with which "Ghost House" begins—a cellar hole on an abandoned farm—was part of the landscape adjacent to the Frost farm. Frost passed by this landmark often on his walks over the countryside. It was located halfway between the house of his closest neighbor, Napoleon Guay, and Klein's hill, just beyond the stone wall on the farm's southern property line.

The house had belonged to Marshall Merriam, who owned most of the land that became the Frost farm. It burned down in 1867, and all that remained of it in Frost's day was a tall chimney standing in an old cellar hole, a scene he transformed into the "vanished" house of the poem.

The visual images Frost creates are grounded in the realistic details of how nature goes about reclaiming a deserted farm. They include the "purple-stemmed wild raspberries" growing in the cellar hole, the grape vines covering the "ruined fences," the mowing field overgrown with trees, and the black bats tumbling and darting in the dark of night. In the fourth verse, sight gives way to sound with the "shout" and "clutter" and "flutter" of the whippoorwill. Frost's eyes and ears were "very open" indeed.

In another context, Frost once said that "a poem is best read in the light of all the other poems ever written." This is a surprising statement coming from a poet who prided himself on being as free as possible from the influence of the writers who came before him. It does not apply to most of Frost's poetry, but as he himself admitted, he was to some extent dependent on the poetry he had read, especially in his early poems. "Ghost House" is an example of his indebtedness to several predecessors. Its melancholy mood and somewhat self-indulgent sentiments are reminiscent of the British romantic poets he had read in his favorite book, Francis Palgrave's *Golden Treasury*. "I *did* read that literally to rags and tatters," he wrote in reply to an admirer's request for a list of his favorite authors.

Echoes of Alfred Lord Tennyson and William Butler Yeats have also been detected in the poem's "sweetly sorrowful" tone. But even here, where literary influences are strongest, Frost succeeds in making the poem distinctly his own. Reginald Cook calls it a "moving and nonsentimental" image of back country New England at the turn of the century. It is an eloquent elegy to a deserted farm, whose downfall has been "decline by defeat and abandonment by default." Cook identifies loneliness as "a central spring in Frost's poetic impulse." In this poem "loneliness is not only a token of place, it is an attribution of the Yankee condition."

Another reader, Mordecai Marcus, interprets the setting differently. To him, the speaker is projecting himself "into a distant scene, either created by imagination or retrieved by memory." He focuses on the last two stanzas where "the speaker summons back departed figures . . . the dead whose names appear on the gravestones." The poem shows a longing for the past and "for an elusive ideal."

Ultimately "Ghost House" is more significant as a harbinger of poems to come than in its own right. It is the first of Frost's poems to use the key images of the deserted landscape and the abandoned house. These two thematically related symbols reoccur in subsequent poems— two of his most critically acclaimed pieces, "The Wood-Pile, " published in 1914, and "Directive," published in 1946, adapt the motif introduced here. In the later poems, Frost develops the concepts more completely within a style that is indebted to no one but himself.

Ghost House

I DWELL in a lonely house I know
That vanished many a summer ago,
 And left no trace but the cellar walls,
 And a cellar in which the daylight falls,
And the purple-stemmed wild raspberries grow.

O'er ruined fences the grape-vines shield
The woods come back to the mowing field;
 The orchard tree has grown one copse
 Of new wood and old where the woodpecker chops;
The footpath down to the well is healed.

I dwell with a strangely aching heart
In that vanished abode there far apart
 On that disused and forgotten road
 That has no dust-bath now for the toad.
Night comes; the black bats tumble and dart;

The whippoorwill is coming to shout
And hush and cluck and flutter about:
 I hear him begin far enough away
 Full many a time to say his say
Before he arrives to say it out.

It is under the small, dim, summer star,
I know not who these mute folk are
 Who share the unlit place with me —
 Those stones out under the low-limbed tree
Doubtless bear names that the mosses mar.

They are tireless folk, but slow and sad,
Though two, close-keeping, are lass and lad, —
 With none among them that ever sings,
 And yet, in view of how many things,
As sweet companions as might be had.

11

Rose Pogonias

In 1905, six-year-old Lesley Frost wrote in her journal about a Sunday walk she and her father took along the old South Road to the cranberry bog on their neighbor's property. They took off their shoes and stockings and waded in to pick the flowers that grew there. Snakemouth was one of the blooms they gathered, a variety of wild orchid classified botanically as Rose Pogonia. The father/daughter adventure is but one of many expeditions Frost took into the swampy regions of New England in search of wild orchids. Carl Burell, who was living and working on the Derry farm when Frost wrote the poem in 1901, introduced Frost to the fun of finding and identifying wildflowers back in 1896.

In "Rose Pogonias," Frost is drawing on a composite of personal experiences, but he is also borrowing from the poets who came before him. The style and tone echo the works of Spenser, Marvell, Wordsworth, and Thoreau, as well as the nineteenth-century women writers who popularized the "language of gems and flowers." Frost usually dismissed the question of how his reading influenced his poetry as irrelevant. "I don't see much meaning in it at all," he said. Yet he did acknowledge, in one essay, that both a poet's life and a poet's reading shape his writing:

> Now the manner of a poet's germination is less like that of a bean in the ground than of a waterspout at sea. He has to begin as a cloud of all the other poets he ever read. That can't be helped. And first the cloud reaches down toward the water from above and then the water reaches up toward the cloud from below and finally cloud and water join together to roll as one pillar between heaven and earth. The base of water he picks up from below is of course all the life he ever lived outside of books.

He also admitted: "When I first began to write poetry . . . I was writing largely, though not exclusively, after the pattern of the past."

He added: "It is only when he [the poet] has outgrown the pattern, and sees clearly for himself his own way that he has really started to become."

In this poem Frost has not yet come into his own, but it shows him flexing his poetic muscle, preparing the way for the voice that will be unmistakably his.

Rose Pogonias

A SATURATED meadow,
  Sun-shaped and jewel-small,
A circle scarcely wider
  Than the trees around were tall;
Where winds were quite excluded,
  And the air was stifling sweet
With the breath of many flowers, —
  A temple of the heat.

There we bowed us in the burning,
  As the sun's right worship is,
To pick where none could miss them
  A thousand orchises;
For though the grass was scattered,
  Yet every second spear
Seemed tipped with wings of color,
  That tinged the atmosphere.

We raised a simple prayer
  Before we left the spot,
That in the general mowing
  That place might be forgot;
Or if not all so favoured,
  Obtain such grace of hours,
That none should mow the grass there
  While so confused with flowers.

12

October

❦

October is the month of "leaf-peepers" in New England. Each autumn, the glorious reds and yellows of the falling leaves beckon to visitors, and the roads and inns are filled to capacity for the seasonal performance. Long before tourists discovered the beauty of autumn in New Hampshire and Vermont, Robert Frost recorded his appreciation in the poem he called "October."

He wrote it in 1901 on the Derry farm. The grapes "along the wall," for whose sake the speaker wants to delay the killing frost, belonged to one of Frost's neighbors, Nathaniel Head. Head built a retaining wall to buttress a steep downward slope on his property adjoining Frost's farm, then planted Concord grapevines along the wall.

In 1912, when this poem was published, Frost was teaching at the state normal school in Plymouth, New Hampshire. Biographer Jay Parini believes Frost revised the poem in the fall of 1911 when he was spending many evenings reading the poetry of W. B. Yeats aloud to Sidney Cox, a young admirer who was teaching at the local high school. The wistfulness and form of the poem may have been influenced by Yeats' verse, yet the playful request that the trees release their leaves slowly, one at a time, is unmistakably Frost. He was, even that early in his career, a "highly distinct and original poet." Frost's half-joking stance is confirmed by the original title he gave the poem, "Determined." His use of the word "beguile" suggests he knows he's asking to be fooled by the charm of October's enchantment. Lawrance Thompson credits the "humor" in the poem with balancing the sadness and keeping the tone from being romantically sentimental.

At one public reading of "October," Frost said, "If you want me to tell you something personal about the poem, I was very much aware that I was giving it a prayer sound." At what turned out to be his last reading in December 1962, he used it as an example of his life-long determination to assign a place "apart" to poetry. Poetry, he said, was something "in itself," "song in itself," above the "contentions" of politics and religion. "October" was such a poem: "innocent of everything I know of." Contemporary admirers of New England's fall foliage will find in it a universal response to nature that transcends the "contentions" of time and place.

October

O HUSHED October morning mild,
Thy leaves have ripened to the fall;
To-morrow's wind, if it be wild,
Should waste them all.
The crows above the forest call;
To-morrow they may form and go.
O hushed October morning mild,
Begin the hours of this day slow,
Make the day seem to us less brief.
Hearts not averse to being beguiled,
Beguile us in the way you know;
Release one leaf at break of day;
At noon release another leaf;
One from our trees, one far away;
Retard the sun with gentle mist;
Enchant the land with amethyst.
Slow, slow!
For the grapes' sake, if they were all,
Whose leaves already are burnt with frost,
Whose clustered fruit must else be lost—
For the grapes' sake along the wall.

13

A Prayer in Spring

"A Prayer in Spring" is literally a poem about the birds and the bees, symbols of the rebirth associated with springtime. It rejoices in the here and now of the New England spring with its apple blossoms and meteor-like hummingbirds.

This poem is also a prayer, a rare phenomenon in Robert Frost's poetry. The question of whether Frost believed in a benevolent God remains a central controversy among Frost scholars, with opinions ranging from defiant "no's" to righteous "yes's," with all gradations of "sometimes" in between. Frost never belonged to any church, and many of his poems express a bitter skepticism. In later years, he often ended his poetry readings with a wry joke of a prayer: "Forgive, O Lord, my little jokes on Thee/ And I'll forgive Thy great big one on me." But as he also said, "I'm never so serious except when I'm fooling." The facts are that as a child he was firmly indoctrinated by his Presbyterian-Unitarian-Swedenborgian mother. As a young man, he classified himself as a "re-thinker" of conventional religious thought rather than a "follower" or an "enemy." And as an adult, he declared (once again in a joking tone): "I discovered that do or say my dambdest I can't be other than orthodox in politics love and religion: I can't escape salvation."

When Robert Frost wrote "A Prayer in Spring" in 1903 on the Derry farm, he must have been experiencing a salvation of sorts. He had arrived there in October 1900 in a state of near-suicidal depression, overwhelmed by sorrow, guilt, fear, and failure. His mother was dying of cancer; he blamed himself for the death of his young son Elliott from cholera; he feared his chronic respiratory problems were developing into the tuberculosis that had killed his father; and he was barely supporting his family after his withdrawal from Harvard. Two-and-a-half years later, the spring that had reinvigorated the flora and fauna on the farm was a mirror image for the new life the Frosts had forged in New Hampshire. A new son, Carol, was born in 1902, and another daughter, Irma, would arrive in June. The grief had subsided,

Frost found he enjoyed chicken farming and being at home with Elinor and the children, and he was writing poetry again.

It is little wonder that one of the poems he wrote took the form of a prayer that rejoices in the pleasures of springtime and the fulfillment of love that it symbolizes.

A Prayer in Spring

Oh, give us pleasure in the flowers to-day;
And give us not to think so far away
As the uncertain harvest; keep us here
All simply in the springing of the year.

Oh, give us pleasure in the orchard white,
Like nothing else by day, like ghosts by night;
And make us happy in the happy bees,
The swarm dilating round the perfect trees.

And make us happy in the darting bird
That suddenly above the bees is heard,
The meteor that thrusts in with needle bill,
And off a blossom in mid air stands still.

For this is love, and nothing else is love,
The which it is reserved for God above
To sanctify to what far ends He will,
But which it only needs that we fulfil.

14

My November Guest

Robert Frost called this poem "a pleasant reminder of the days when the clouds were just beginning to break," a reference to the time when he wrote it, in 1903 on the Derry farm. By then the Frosts had come to terms with the death of Elliott in 1900. In the intervening years, their household had grown; four-year-old Lesley now had a one-year-old brother, Carol, and a new baby sister, Irma. The farm was not making money, but, Frost remembered, "We had plenty to eat." He was adapting the routine of farm chores so he could write poetry during the quiet night hours. And most significantly of all, he was beginning to find his poetic voice.

This is one of Frost's earliest attempts to write a "talk song," a conscious effort to incorporate the "sound of sense" into his poetry. He once used this poem to demonstrate his new technique. In a letter to his friend and former student John Bartlett, he wrote: "Take My November Guest. Did you know at once how we say such sentences as this when we talk?

> She thinks I have no eyes for these.
> Not yesterday I learned etc.
> But it were vain to tell her so."

These lines, Frost explained, were "definite entities . . . apprehended by the ear." They were examples of sentence sounds that "often say more than the words."

Poetics aside, it is Elinor Frost who dominates this poem. It is addressed to her, sorrow being an emotion Frost associated with her all his life. After Elinor's death, he wrote to his daughter Lesley: "sorrow runs through all she wrote to you children. No wonder something of it overcasts my poetry." Echoing Frost's debt to Elinor, the speaker in the poem credits his "Sorrow" with enabling him to appreciate the stark beauty "of bare November days. " Frost's acknowledgment goes further: Elinor, he said, was "the unspoken half of everything I ever wrote," and in "My November Guest" she was "both halves."

Frost was modest about this poem. In 1912, he admitted it was not "a new force in literature" but simply "a beginning—that is all." But it was an important beginning, another step toward what would become Frost's distinctive style.

My November Guest

MY Sorrow, when she's here with me,
  Thinks these dark days of autumn rain
Are beautiful as days can be;
She loves the bare, the withered tree;
  She walks the sodden pasture lane.

Her pleasure will not let me stay.
  She talks and I am fain to list:
She's glad the birds are gone away,
She's glad her simple worsted grey
  Is silver now with clinging mist.

The desolate, deserted trees,
  The faded earth, the heavy sky,
The beauties she so truly sees,
She thinks I have no eye for these,
  And vexes me for reason why.

Not yesterday I learned to know
  The love of bare November days,
Before the coming of the snow,
But it were vain to tell her so,
  And they are better for her praise.

15

A Time to Talk

Early in Robert Frost's career, someone told him that reading his poetry was like hearing him talk. Frost credited that casual observation with changing the whole course of his writing. He explained: "I didn't know until then what I was after. When he said that to me, it all became clear. I was after poetry that talked." This poem about talking is a good example of what Frost meant by "talking poems."

He would eventually come to call his attempt to capture the cadence of human speech in his poetry "the sound of sense," but in 1905, when he wrote "A Time to Talk," he had not yet coined the phrase. Nevertheless, this poem illustrates how Frost practiced what later became one of the most important principles in his theory of poetics. He believed that poetry should mesh meter, rhythm, and rhyme with the flow of conversation, thereby giving the poem "the abstract vitality of our speech." In this poem, Frost controls the tension between the firm beat of the measured lines and "the odd arrest and flow of American country speech." Reuben Brower points out that Frost counts on our being familiar with the phrase "What is it?" We inflect it according to how we remember hearing it and are then prepared for the rhyming "visit" in the last line.

This poem captures two of the stereotypes associated with New Englanders—the close-lipped, hard-working, and independent loner as well as the supportive good neighbor always ready to swap a tale with a friend. When the speaker takes time out to talk, he favors the second over the first. Communication is central to the poem. Even the slowed-down pace of the horse "to a meaning walk" communicates the rider's wish to the farmer. He wants to stop and talk.

The stone wall in the poem establishes the Derry farm setting. A stone wall marked the edge of Frost's property. One of his neighbors in 1905 may also have prompted Frost to write a poem about taking time to talk. John Hall was a nearby poultry farmer who initially caught Frost's attention because of his prize-winning chickens. Frost soon came to appreciate him more, however, for his quick wit, picturesque vocabulary, and a Yankee way of speaking that peppered his words with telling intonations and pauses. Frost was intrigued by Hall's talking style and gradually began to incorporate his idioms and rhythms into his own speech. Frost's original biographer, Lawrance Thompson, said Frost was "perfecting the art of talking like a farmer." More significantly, he was writing like one.

Between 1903 and 1905, Frost wrote a series of stories about chicken farming that were, in attitude and voice, characteristic of New England farmers. One of them was about John Hall. A total of eight prose pieces were published in poultry journals, but the poetry he was also writing during these years was not getting published. In fact, "A Time to Talk" did not appear in print until 1916.

The speaker's decision to take time to talk turned out to be a prophetic move for Frost because he became one of the most famous conversationalists of the twentieth century. Frost was "brilliant, provocative, learned, and original," according to Peter J. Stanlis, who heard and saw him in action. Throughout his life, Frost never hesitated to find "a time to talk," and his friends were the better for it.

A Time to Talk

When a friend calls to me from the road
And slows his horse to a meaning walk,
I don't stand still and look around
On all the hills I haven't hoed,
And shout from where I am, What is it?
No, not as there is a time to talk.
I thrust my hoe in the mellow ground,
Blade-end up and five feet tall,
And plod: I go up to the stone wall
For a friendly visit.

16

Putting in the Seed

"Putting in the Seed" begins with the everyday words of a New England farmer asking his wife to come back to "fetch" him "when supper's on the table." But before the poem is ended, the ordinary talk of rural folk has been elevated to poetic language in a song of celebration about the joy of procreation.

When Robert Frost wrote this sonnet in 1905, he knew first hand about both kinds of insemination, about putting seeds in the earth and about fathering babies. He had planted five gardens since the move to New Hampshire in the fall of 1900. And his wife had given birth to three children at the farm—a son, Carol, in 1902, and two daughters, Irma in 1903 and Marjorie in 1905. Frost often referred to these first five years on the Derry farm as "the most sacred in his entire life," crediting them with a seminal role in his development as a poet. It was a fertile time on several levels—for growing vegetables, conceiving babies, and writing poems.

Frost addresses all three creative processes, using the farmer's tilling of the soil as the impetus for his intense engagement in the earth's seasonal cycle of gestation and birth. The passion he feels propels him into telling the woman he loves about his newly found ecstasy, using words that reverberate with the conjugal intimacy that brought new life into their lives.

Jeffrey Meyers calls this "one of Frost's most sensual poems . . . The man puts the seed in the woman as well as in the ground . . . the birth of the child follows naturally from the arched bodies in the sexual act. The infant shoulders its way out of the womb and into the world just as a new seed comes alive by pushing through the earth." Frost, who on one occasion said, "Yes, I suppose I am a Puritan," would most likely not have approved of Meyer's interpretation. Richard Poirier's less explicit, but equally insightful commentary would probably have been more to his liking. Poirier sees it as a poem about a man who "joins creatively in a process that unites the human body and its transformations with the earth and its changes."

Putting in the Seed

You come to fetch me from my work to-night
When supper's on the table, and we'll see
If I can leave off burying the white
Soft petals fallen from the apple tree.

(Soft petals, yes, but not so barren quite,
Mingled with these, smooth bean and wrinkled pea;)
And go along with you ere you lose sight
Of what you came for and become like me,

Slave to a springtime passion for the earth.
How Love burns through the Putting in the Seed
On through the watching for that early birth
When, just as the soil tarnishes with weed,

The sturdy seedling with arched body comes
Shouldering its way and shedding the earth's crumbs.

17

Going for Water

"I never invent for poetic expression," Robert Frost said. "It is all fact." His statement rings true in "Going for Water," whose setting and story are rooted in the facts of Frost's life in 1905, when he wrote it. He and Elinor were living in the Derry farmhouse with a well beside the door, a field behind the house, and a brook in their nearby woods, just as described in the opening verses. Pails and cans stood by for emergency trips to their brook, but it often ran out of water by the end of summer too. Just as the couple in the poem does not appear unduly concerned about the water problem, Frost and Elinor usually ignored the discomforts of rural living. They focused their attention on the natural beauty around them and enjoyed the freedom and privacy they found there. Frost called the years on the Derry farm between 1900 and 1905 his "five free years." "The only thing we had plenty of was time and seclusion," he said in retrospect, "But it turned out right as a doctor's prescription."

This poem also confirms another claim Frost made: "All poetry is to me first a matter of sound." The last two verses of "Going for Water" illustrate how important auditory images are in his poems. He prepares for the sound of the brook by creating an absence of sound in the "hush" that precedes it. Frost's "ear for silences" was noted in a review of *A Boy's Will*, where this poem appeared in print for the first time in 1913. Frost enhances the effect of the silence with the repetitive "We heard, we knew we heard" that adds emphasis and suspense.

It was this "hearing imagination rather than the seeing imagination" that Frost valued, but he added, "I should not want to be without the latter." The visual imagery in the last two lines is striking, leading one critic to find a confluence of feminine and masculine configurations in the passive drops and the assertive blade. The two images, though separate, are parts of the same "slender tinkling fall," mirroring the union of the man and woman who share the magical moonlight romp to the brook.

Going for Water

The well was dry beside the door,
 And so we went with pail and can
Across the fields behind the house
 To seek the brook if still it ran;

Not loth to have excuse to go,
 Because the autumn eve was fair
(Though chill), because the fields were ours,
 And by the brook our woods were there.

We ran as if to meet the moon
 That slowly dawned behind the trees,
The barren boughs without the leaves,
 Without the birds, without the breeze.

But once within the wood, we paused
 Like gnomes that hid us from the moon,
Ready to run to hiding new
 With laughter when she found us soon.

Each laid on other a staying hand
 To listen ere we dared to look,
And in the hush we joined to make
 We heard, we knew we heard the brook.

A note as from a single place,
 A slender tinkling fall that made
Now drops that floated on the pool
 Like pearls, and now a silver blade.

18

The Death of the Hired Man

The grim title of this poem is misleading. The death of Silas, the hired man, provides the dramatic climax, but the main concept of the poem is not about dying—it is about loving. Two kinds of life-affirming love are involved. The first is the love of one's neighbor (in the biblical sense), and the second is the love between husband and wife, a force for conciliation between two often opposing points-of-view.

When Robert Frost wrote this poem in 1905, he was living an almost idyllic life as a farmer-poet. Neither his farming nor his poetry was bringing in enough money to pay the bills, however, and by the spring of 1906 he began teaching at Pinkerton Academy. The "time-rich" days on the farm were over, but not before he had written a tribute to married love in the poem he chose to call "The Death of the Hired Man."

The title character, Silas, represented for Frost a type of New Englander he had come to know well. During a talk he gave fifty-five years after he wrote this poem, he reminisced, "I always wanted to do something about the kind of American hired man that I'd lived with and worked with and been." When Frost was fifteen, and again when he was seventeen, he was hired to work on a haying crew. In his description of young Harold Wilson as a student who learned Latin just because he liked it, he could well have been thinking of his own love of Latin in high school. One hired man Frost lived and worked with was his old high-school friend Carl Burell, who worked for him between 1900 and 1902. Carl took the job on condition his grandfather could live on the farm with him and be allowed to do some chores. The increasingly feeble man died on the farm in 1902, perhaps suggesting the poem's climax.

This is one of Frost's first dramatic poems, different from the lyric poetry he had been writing. It is longer and features a narrator who uses dialogue to tell a story about other people. Frost spoke of it as "a little drama in which the gradual change in Warren is shown. It has four distinctly drawn characters. It has climax and surprise; and it perfectly observes all the old unities." He had read what Aristotle had to say about the unities of time, place, and action, and he adhered to them.

What he thought was important in the poem, however, was something else: he said he wanted attention paid to "the way in which the sentences suggest the tones." He used the passage in which Mary tries to get Warren to lower his voice as an example. Once, in a discussion about voice tones, Frost quoted from a speech by the Lady in John Milton's poem *Comus*: "Shall I go on? / Or have I said enough?" After repeating the phrases, he commented: "I like to think of it as two such lovely tones of inquiry. And that's what I think makes poetry." Reginald Cook recalled that in speaking the Miltonic lines, Frost gave each question its special emphasis just as he gave distinctive human tonalities to the words and lines in the speeches in "The Death of the Hired Man."

On November 27, 1915, Frost saw a staged performance of this poem that disturbed and upset him. The actors who portrayed Mary and Warren spoke their lines crudely and stomped about the stage clumsily in what appeared to be an attempt to convey the characters' country backgrounds. Frost was furious and went backstage to angrily accuse the actors of not understanding his characters. Warren was not a fool or a clodhopper, and both Warren and Mary were intelligent, college-educated people. In retelling how his poem had been misread, Frost added "the danger is that you shall make the man [Warren] too hard. That spoils it . . . all our thinking turns on that."

This rare bit of advice from Frost on how to read his poem warns us not to accept either Warren's or Mary's view as the "right" one. Their outlooks are not meant to be examples of bad versus good; rather they are what Frost elsewhere calls "opposing goods." In their appraisals of Silas, Warren adheres to the logic of justice and discipline while Mary follows her heart. She advocates mercy toward the old man, who, in spite of his shortcomings, is trying to hang on to his last shred of dignity and self-respect. In their famous contrasting definitions of home, Frost explained that Mary's view is "the feminine way of it, the mother way. You don't have to deserve your mother's love. You have to deserve your father's."

In the skillfully constructed dialogue between Mary and Warren, the feminine way, drawing on the reservoir of tenderness their love has created, gradually succeeds in getting the masculine way to temper justice with mercy. In the words of an early reviewer, the poem is one of Frost's "masterpieces of deep and mysterious tenderness." Frost himself said this was a poem in which he was sure he had "got something he was after."

The Death of the Hired Man

Mary sat musing on the lamp-flame at the table
Waiting for Warren. When she heard his step,
She ran on tip-toe down the darkened passage
To meet him in the doorway with the news
And put him on his guard. "Silas is back."
She pushed him outward with her through the door
And shut it after her. "Be kind," she said.
She took the market things from Warren's arms
And set them on the porch, then drew him down
To sit beside her on the wooden steps.

"When was I ever anything but kind to him?
But I'll not have the fellow back," he said.
"I told him so last haying, didn't I?
'If he left then,' I said, 'that ended it.'
 What good is he? Who else will harbour him
At his age for the little he can do?
What help he is there's no depending on.
Off he goes always when I need him most.
'He thinks he ought to earn a little pay,
Enough at least to buy tobacco with,
So he won't have to beg and be beholden.'
'All right,' I say, 'I can't afford to pay
Any fixed wages, though I wish I could.'
'Someone else can.' 'Then someone else will have to.'
I shouldn't mind his bettering himself
If that was what it was. You can be certain,
when he begins like that, there's someone at him
Trying to coax him off with pocket-money,—
In haying time, when any help is scarce.
In winter he comes back to us. I'm done."

"Sh! not so loud: he'll hear you," Mary said.

"I want him to: he'll have to soon or late."

"He's worn out. He's asleep beside the stove.
When I came up from Rowe's I found him here,
Huddled against the barn-door fast asleep,
A miserable sight, and frightening, too—
You needn't smile—I didn't recognise him—
I wasn't looking for him—and he's changed.
Wait till you see."

          "Where did you say he'd been?"

"He didn't say. I dragged him to the house,
And gave him tea and tried to make him smoke.
I tried to make him talk about his travels.
Nothing would do: he just kept nodding off."

"What did he say? Did he say anything?"

"But little."

                    "Anything? Mary, confess
He said he'd come to ditch the meadow for me."

"Warren!"

                    "But did he? I just want to know."

"Of course he did. What would you have him say?
Surely you wouldn't grudge the poor old man
Some humble way to save his self-respect.
He added, if you really care to know,
He meant to clear the upper pasture, too.
That sounds like something you have heard before?
Warren, I wish you could have heard the way

He jumbled everything. I stopped to look
Two or three times—he made me feel so queer—
To see if he was talking in his sleep.
He ran on Harold Wilson—you remember—
The boy you had in haying four years since.
He's finished school, and teaching in his college.
Silas declares you'll have to get him back.
He says they two will make a team for work:
Between them they will lay this farm as smooth!
The way he mixed that in with other things.
He thinks young Wilson a likely lad, though daft
On education—you know how they fought
All through July under the blazing sun,
Silas up on the cart to build the load,
Harold along beside to pitch it on."

"Yes, I took care to keep well out of earshot."

"Well, those days trouble Silas like a dream.
You wouldn't think they would. How some things linger!
Harold's young college boy's assurance piqued him.
After so many years he still keeps finding
Good arguments he sees he might have used.
I sympathise. I know just how it feels
To think of the right thing to say too late.
Harold's associated in his mind with Latin.
He asked me what I thought of Harold's saying
He studied Latin like the violin
Because he liked it—that an argument!
He said he couldn't make the boy believe
He could find water with a hazel prong—
Which showed how much good school had ever done him.
He wanted to go over that. But most of all
He thinks if he could have another chance

To teach him how to build a load of hay——"

"I know, that's Silas' one accomplishment.
He bundles every forkful in its place,
And tags and numbers it for future reference,
So he can find and easily dislodge it
In the unloading. Silas does that well.
He takes it out in bunches like big birds' nests.
You never see him standing on the hay
He's trying to lift, straining to lift himself."

"He thinks if he could teach him that, he'd be
Some good perhaps to someone in the world.
He hates to see a boy the fool of books.
Poor Silas, so concerned for other folk,
And nothing to look backward to with pride,
And nothing to look forward to with hope,
So now and never any different."

Part of a moon was falling down the west,
Dragging the whole sky with it to the hills.
Its light poured softly in her lap. She saw
And spread her apron to it. She put out her hand
Among the harp-like morning-glory strings,
Taut with the dew from garden bed to eaves,
As if she played unheard the tenderness
That wrought on him beside her in the night.
"Warren," she said, "he has come home to die:
You needn't be afraid he'll leave you this time."

"Home," he mocked gently.

                              "Yes, what else but home?
It all depends on what you mean by home.
Of course he's nothing to us, any more

Than was the hound that came a stranger to us
Out of the woods, worn out upon the trail."

"Home is the place where, when you have to go there,
They have to take you in."

                    "I should have called it
Something you somehow haven't to deserve."

 Warren leaned out and took a step or two,
Picked up a little stick, and brought it back
And broke it in his hand and tossed it by.
"Silas has better claim on us you think
Than on his brother? Thirteen little miles
As the road winds would bring him to his door.
Silas has walked that far no doubt to-day.
Why didn't he go there? His brother's rich,
A somebody—director in the bank."

"He never told us that."

                    "We knew it though."

"I think his brother ought to help, of course.
I'll see to that if there is need. He ought of right
To take him in, and might be willing to—
He may be better than appearances.
But have some pity on Silas. Do you think
If he'd had any pride in claiming kin
Or anything he looked for from his brother,
He'd keep so still about him all this time?"

"I wonder what's between them."

                    "I can tell you.
Silas is what he is—we wouldn't mind him—

But just the kind that kinsfolk can't abide.
He never did a thing so very bad.
He don't know why he isn't quite as good
As anyone. He won't be made ashamed
To please his brother, worthless though he is."

"I can' t think Si ever hurt anyone."

"No, but he hurt my heart the way he lay
And rolled his old head on that sharp-edged chair-back.
He wouldn't let me put him on the lounge.
You must go in and see what you can do.
I made a bed up for him there to-night.
You'll be surprised at him—how much he's broken.
His working days are done; I'm sure of it."

"I'd not be in a hurry to say that."

"I haven't been. Go, look, see for yourself.
But, Warren, please remember how it is:
He's come to help you ditch the meadow.
He has a plan. You mustn't laugh at him.
He may not speak of it, and then he may.
I'll sit and see if that small sailing cloud
Will hit or miss the moon."

                    It hit the moon.
Then there were three there, making a dim row,
The moon, the little silver cloud, and she.

Warren returned—too soon, it seemed to her,
Slipped to her side, caught up her hand and waited.

"Warren," she questioned.

                  "Dead," was all he answered.

19

Pea Brush

Most readers have no idea what the title of this poem means. The term refers to the brushwood used in staking pea plants. Robert Frost must have been serious when he claimed that "all life is a fit subject for poetic treatment." That included what he saw and heard and felt as he walked to a neighbor's clearing to collect newly cut birch boughs for his peas.

Frost began this poem in 1905, drawing once again on the mundane details of his life on the Derry farm. Like much of the poetry Frost wrote during these years, it became part of the sheafs of poems he held on to for a long time before submitting them for publication. He said it was in Derry that "I wrote more than half of my first book much more than half of my second and even quite a little of my third, though they were not published till later." This poem falls into the last of these categories. Frost held it until 1916, when it became part of his third book, *Mountain Interval.*

A four-stanza draft titled "Pea-sticks" did make an informal public appearance two years earlier, however, in the July 1914 edition of *The Bouquet,* a typewritten magazine put together by the Frost children while the family was living in England. Its author was identified as "Anon."

In a copy of *Mountain Interval* that Frost gave his biographer, Lawrance Thompson, he inscribed lines 5 to 12 of the final six-stanza version, adding the phrase "A Spring Day in a New Clearing." The caption broadens the poem's significance and offers an alternate title for readers whose personal experience might not include staking pea plants in a spring garden.

The trillium in the last verse is another example of Frost's accurate rendition of the flora of New England. Frost saw a lot of trillium in his walks in New Hampshire. He and his children transplanted two varieties of it to the flower beds along the porch and under the bay window of the Derry farmhouse. "The land is always in my bones," Frost said. The specific objects in nature he chose to write about in realistic detail affirm his kinship with the New England landscape.

Pea Brush

I walked down alone Sunday after church
 To the place where John has been cutting trees
To see for myself about the birch
 He said I could have to bush my peas.

The sun in the new-cut narrow gap
 Was hot enough for the first of May.
And stifling hot with the odor of sap
 From stumps still bleeding their life away.

The frogs that were peeping a thousand shrill
 Wherever the ground was low and wet,
The minute they hear my step went still
 To watch me and see what I came to get.

Birch boughs enough piled everywhere!—
 All fresh and sound from the recent axe.
Time someone came with cart and pair
 And got them off the wild flowers' backs.

They might be good for garden things
 To curl a little finger round,
The same as you seize cat's-cradle strings,
 And lift themselves up off the ground.

Small good to anything growing wild,
 They were crooking many a trillium
That had budded before the boughs were piled
 And since it was coming up had to come.

20

The Oven Bird

Anyone taking a summer walk through the New England woods today is likely to hear the raucous song of the oven bird. Robert Frost heard it often on his walks through the New Hampshire countryside when he was a chicken farmer. According to Peterson's *Field Guide to the Birds*, the oven bird belongs to an "aberrant species" of sparrow-sized warblers, more often heard than seen because of the olive-brown coloring that blends them with the floor of the woods where they walk. Long after the orioles and thrushes have stopped singing their melodious songs in mid-summer, the oven bird's shrill insistent call fills the woods; "*teach'er*, TEACH'ER, *TEACH'ER*" it shrieks rapidly in crescendo. Frost mimics this distinctive sound by repeating "He says" three times, at the beginning of each of the sentences in the middle seven lines of the poem.

He was in his mid-thirties in 1906 and 1907 when he wrote this sonnet about the odd-sounding bird, whose equally odd name comes from its oven-shaped nest. The adjectives he uses to describe the bird, "mid-summer" and "mid-wood," are reminiscent of the opening lines of Dante's *Inferno*, where Dante at thirty-five—traditionally the half-way mark in life—finds himself lost in the middle of the woods. Like Dante, Frost's youth is behind him as he moves through the "highway dust" of summer into the early fall of middle age. It is this falling off from the full springtime bloom of things that seems to have prompted the poem, along with its final question: what to make of such diminished things?

The answer, according to one reader, is to "make" a poem out of them. That is what Frost does, thereby implying a bittersweet acceptance and the need to persist. Another admirer once addressed Frost as "Dear Oven Bird," suggesting that Frost was writing about himself as a singer of poems. Reginald Cook, who knew Frost well, concurs when he claims this is one of Frost's parables. Like the bird's song, Frost's poetry sounds like human speech, making him as different from other poets as the oven bird is from "other birds." In a letter advocating the use of "sentence sounds" caught "fresh from talk," he included a piece of advice that helps to explain one of the contradictions in this poem. Frost warned: "Get away from the sing-song." Like the oven bird, the good poet "knows in singing not to sing."

The Oven Bird

There is a singer everyone has heard,
Loud, a mid-summer and a mid-wood bird,
Who makes the solid tree trunks sound again.
He says that leaves are old and that for flowers
Mid-summer is to spring as one to ten.
He says the early petal-fall is past
When pear and cherry bloom went down in showers
On sunny days a moment overcast;
And comes that other fall we name the fall.
He says the highway dust is over all.
The bird would cease and be as other birds
But that he knows in singing not to sing.
The question that he frames in all but words
Is what to make of a diminished thing.

21

An Old Man's Winter Night

At first glance, "An Old Man's Winter Night" has the makings of a Norman Rockwell *Saturday Evening Post* cover. A cozy cabin nestles in the New England woods, its roof covered with snow and fringed with icicles. The moonlight streams in one of the lightly frosted windows to highlight the figure of an aged man, seated next to a wood-burning stove and nodding off to sleep, an image from a simpler and more serene time.

But a closer look quickly dispels the surface appearance of sentimental nostalgia. This is a desolate, lonely, confused, and frightened old man. His taciturn, Yankee kind of stubbornness allows him to accept an isolated existence that would kill less hardy souls. He survives the winter night—and his winter life—with a measure of dignity.

When Robert Frost wrote this poem during the winter of 1906-1907, he was living on the Derry farm in a bustling household with a wife and four children. The summer before, on August 3, 1906, the *Derry Enterprise* had run a story about a local man, Charles Lambert, who lived in the area for years as a hermit. Frost unflinchingly portrays the bleakness of such a life, which was so different from his own.

But there is much about the anonymous old man in the poem that Frost identifies with too. He could understand being afraid of the dark, a fear he had lived with since childhood. As late as high school, he still slept on a cot in his mother's room. He lived alone for the first time in his life during the summer of 1895 on Ossipee Mountain in New Hampshire, in a cabin suspiciously like the one in the poem. It was a "forest-shrouded," forlorn cottage "with uncurtained windows." The only habitable room was the kitchen, which featured a potbellied cast-iron stove, and the cellar held "several barrels of hard cider." One night, unable to sleep because of strange and inexplicable noises, he lit his lantern and found "comfort" in making noise by firing his pistol at an iron lid he had taken off the stove. Eleven years later, Frost drew on his summer apprehensions as a young man of twenty-one to authentically create the winter terrors of an old man. When it was published in *Mountain Interval* in 1916, Frost thought it was the best poem in the book.

An Old Man's Winter Night

All out of doors looked darkly in at him
Through the thin frost, almost in separate stars,
That gathers on the pane in empty rooms.
What kept his eye from giving back the gaze
Was the lamp tilted near them in his hand.
What kept him from remembering what it was
That brought him to that creaking room was age.
He stood with barrels round him—at a loss.
And having scared the cellar under him
In clomping there, he scared it once again
In clomping off;—and scared the outer night,
Which has its sounds, familiar, like the roar
Of trees and crack of branches, common things,
But nothing so like beating on a box.
A light he was to no one but himself
Where now he sat, concerned with he knew what,
A quiet light, and then not even that.
He consigned to the moon, such as she was,
So late-arising, to the broken moon
As better than the sun in any case
For such a charge, his snow upon the roof,
His icicles along the wall to keep;
And slept. The log that shifted with a jolt
Once in the stove, disturbed him and he shifted,
And eased his heavy breathing, but still slept.
One aged man—one man—can't fill a house,
A farm, a countryside, or if he can,
It's thus he does it of a winter night.

22

Hyla Brook

By late June many of the brooks throughout New England have run out of water, their dry beds dotted with clumps of jewel-weed. Gone too are the "peepers," the small frogs whose chirps in early spring herald the end of winter. Sometime between 1900 and 1912, Robert Frost turned this natural phenomenon into a poem. The exact year has not been established, but he probably wrote "Hyla Brook" in 1906 or 1907, when he was experimenting with sonnets. In 1915 he described it in a letter as "a little poem about the brook on my old farm. It always dried up in summer. The Hyla is a small frog that shouts like jingling bells in the marshes in spring."

The poem's title, and the name he gave to the brook that inspired it, probably came from one of Frost's favorite books, Charles Darwin's *Voyage of the Beagle*, which lists the classifying characteristics of the genus Hyla. Frost's description of the frog's song in the poem—"Like ghost of sleigh-bells in a ghost of snow"—captures the bell-like ringing sound while invoking the memory of winter and the inevitable passing of the seasons. Reuben Brower calls it the "most exquisite line in the poem."

In the next to the last line, Frost contrasts his brook with "brooks taken otherwhere in song," clearly referring to the familiar refrain in Tennyson's "The Brook": "For men may come and men may go,/ But I go on for ever." Unlike the Romantic British poets of the nineteenth century, whose idealized portrayal of nature did not always conform to the actual, Frost's nature is rooted in the factual day-to-day reality of the New England landscape.

Frost claimed that the last line "clinches the metaphor of the poem." For Frost, metaphor was the most important element in poetry, going so far as to say "Poetry is simply made up of metaphor." He defined it in simple terms: "saying one thing and meaning another, saying one thing in terms of another." Through the image of his persevering love for the brook, now a dried-up relic of its former self, the poem says "one thing" about the love of nature, but means "another," pointing to the other world of love for fellow human beings.

Hyla Brook

By June our brook's run out of song and speed.
Sought for much after that, it will be found
Either to have gone groping underground
(And taken with it all the Hyla breed
That shouted in the mist a month ago,
Like ghost of sleigh-bells in a ghost of snow)—
Or flourished and come up in jewel-weed,
Weak foliage that is blown upon and bent
Even against the way its waters went.
Its bed is left a faded paper sheet
Of dead leaves stuck together by the heat—
A brook to none but who remember long.
This as it will be seen is other far
Than with brooks taken otherwhere in song.
We love the things we love for what they are.

23

The Pasture

Robert Frost's farmhouse in Derry, New Hampshire, had a large bay window at the front of the house that looked out on two small pastures. One spring evening in 1905, Frost took a walk over those fields with his wife, Elinor, and their six-year-old daughter, Lesley. According to the notebook Lesley kept as a child, she and her mother picked apple and strawberry blossoms while her father went down to the southwest corner of the big cow pasture to check on how much water was in the spring. In 1910, when Frost wrote "The Pasture," he used a walk to a spring in a cow pasture as its centerpiece. The experience was still a favorite memory thirty years after he wrote about it. In 1940 he reminisced, "I never had a greater pleasure than coming on a neglected spring in a pasture in the woods."

When Frost chose "The Pasture" to be the prologue poem in his second book, *North of Boston*, he clearly meant the "you" in "You come too" to mean the reader. And in his first collected edition, as in those that have followed, it has remained an invitation to the reader to join Frost in his poetic explorations of the New England countryside. Surprising, then, is Frost's assertion that "The Pasture" is a love poem, suggesting that the original "you" was his wife. He went on to explain that it is "a poem about love that's new in treatment and effect. You won't find anything in the range of English poetry just like that." The unique treatment of love in the poem has an intensely personal connection with the long-standing tempestuous relationship between Frost and his wife.

Frost appears to have had misgivings about Elinor's love for him since their courtship days, when she refused to leave St. Lawrence University to marry him. The differences between them and the extent of his doubt and anger are revealed in a dreamlike incident Lesley remembered from when she was six. One night her father woke her, revolver in hand, to ask her to choose between her mother and him, because one of them would be dead by morning. Lesley's brother, Carol, is reputed to have said that Lesley was dreaming and that the incident never happened.

No one ever accused Frost of physically harming his wife, but they did have their quarrels. Frost's usual response was to storm out of the house for long walks alone in the woods, often not returning until after dark. The gentle invitation in the poem asking Elinor to join him on his walk is in striking contrast to the rejection he was expressing every time he walked away from her. The renewals associated with springtime—the reinvigorated pasture spring, the newborn calf—contribute to the poem's plea for another beginning, a rebirth of their togetherness.

Another claim Frost made for this poem was that it could be used "to express the opposite of confusion." He admitted that "confusion" was a word he "always had an interest in." He thought watching "the uncloudiness displace the cloudiness" in the spring could "be taken as a figure of speech" for his goal of seeing "clarity come out of . . . confusion." The passage "And wait to watch the water clear" from the first verse became the epigraph for his last book of poems, *In the Clearing*, published in 1962, the year before he died. At eighty-seven, he was still seeking an "unclouded" vision.

The Pasture

I'm going out to clean the pasture spring;
I'll only stop to rake the leaves away
(And wait to watch the water clear, I may);
I sha'n't be gone long.—You come too.

I'm going out to fetch the little calf
That's standing by the mother. It's so young
It totters when she licks it with her tongue.
I sha'n't be gone long.—You come too.

24

Storm Fear

New England's famed winter storms, with their blowing snow, howling winds, and freezing temperatures, always unsettled Robert Frost. He captures the essence of the storms in this brief ode, based on a blizzard on the Derry farm in late winter 1902.

Line 3 in the poem—"Two and a child"—establishes the time and place in the poem, as Frost, Elinor, and their daughter Lesley were the only ones on the farm for just two months. Carol was born in May 1902, and Carl Burell and his grandfather, who had been living with them and helping with the chores, had left in early March. Frost may have jotted down a few lines of the poem in 1902, but he did not rework the fragments into a full poem until almost a decade later, after the family had moved to Plymouth in 1911.

Frost's fear of storms was pervasive and persistent, and the storm recreated in the poem could well have been a composite of the many snowstorms that were part of the New Hampshire years. One in December 1907 is recorded in Lesley's journal, reflecting the same fears as her father's: "Last night there was a great snow storm outside . . . I didn't want to go to bed because you could hear the wind outside whistling around the corner of the house and coming in every crack in the windows and the fine sharp flakes banging against the window pane. . . . I was afraid I might dream."

When "Storm Fear" was published in 1913 in Frost's first book, *A Boy's Will,* he added a brief explanatory note: "He is afraid of his own isolation." The comment, like the others that accompany the individual poems in the collection, were meant to give the book coherence, each one pointing to a stage in a young man's development. In clarifying the meaning of his notes, he confirms the connection between the speaker in this poem and himself. He explains: "You can never tell which person I am writing under. 'I' sometimes means 'he,' while 'he,' as in this case, means 'I.'" The case he was referring to was the "he" who is afraid of his own isolation in "Storm Fear."

In reflecting on this collection, Frost also said: "I find I don't get over liking the few lyrics I ever really liked in my first book." He mentioned "the one I call Storm Fear" as particularly "interesting as it shades off into the nearly lyrical." He liked this poem's intensity and compression as well; he felt he had never written a "tighter" poem. Others praise its "suppleness of movement" and its subtle yet simple language. According to William Pritchard, the rhythm is enhanced by the rhymes "never quite coming when you expect them," and the precise shades of meaning are achieved in spite of there being "only two words of more than two syllables in the whole of it."

Thematically, "Storm Fear" brings together two of Frost's recurring and related concerns that go beyond the immediate situation: nature as an unfeeling antagonistic force, and the human response of fear and isolation.

Storm Fear

When the wind works against us in the dark,
And pelts with snow
The lower-chamber window in the east,
And whispers with a sort of stifled bark,
The beast,
"Come out! Come out!"—
It costs no inward struggle not to go,
Ah, no!
I count our strength,
Two and a child,
Those of us not asleep subdued to mark
How the cold creeps as the fire dies at length,—
How drifts are piled,
Dooryard and road ungraded,
Till even the comforting barn grows far away,
And my heart owns a doubt
Whether 'tis in us to arise with day
And save ourselves unaided.

25

Good Hours

Robert Frost called this poem "a little stanza of a village evening . . . an old memory of Plymouth." What he was remembering was a walk he took one night during the winter of 1911-12 in Plymouth, New Hampshire. Frost moved there before the fall term, when he was hired as a faculty member at Plymouth Normal School.

He spent an enriching year in Plymouth, a time of transition. He was enjoying the intellectual stimulation of his new teaching post, but as he said later: "I must either teach or write: can't do both together." He explored the possibility of moving his family to Vancouver or England, where they could live inexpensively while he devoted himself to his writing. Nevertheless, he found time to write a few poems in Plymouth, and "Good Hours" was one of them.

The village is a change of setting for Frost's poetry, a reflection of his life at the time he wrote this poem. Frost loved to walk, and the walks he took often inspired poems. In this one, the usual country paths he took through pastures and woods have been replaced by a cottage-lined village street. In some respects, it is a stereotypical calendar scene of a New England town, but with a crucial difference: the point-of-view provided by the speaker. We view the landscape through the eyes of one who is aware of being alone in the midst of the bright lights and sociability he sees in the windows. His observations have an unexpected edge.

Reginald Cook credits Frost with being "a master of the single word" that changes the poem's tone and keeps it from being trite. In "Good Hours" the word is "profanation." It "carries a slyly humorous comment on life in a sleepy back-country village." The down-home "ten o'clock" curfew in the last line confirms the deliberate exaggeration of "profanation" and "repented," words normally associated with sacred things.

This poem was first published in *North of Boston*, where it appeared as the final selection. It serves as a kind of epilogue to the volume he subtitled a "book of people." In that light, the poem could be about the poet's role as observer (an outsider looking in) and as a profaner of people's private lives (he exposes them to public scrutiny when he uses them in his poetry.) If Frost felt any guilt over this, he handles it lightly, the tone and title of the poem belying any serious concern.

Good Hours

I HAD for my winter evening walk—
No one at all with whom to talk,
But I had the cottages in a row
Up to their shining eyes in snow.

And I thought I had the folk within:
I had the sound of a violin;
I had a glimpse through curtain laces
Of youthful forms and youthful faces.

I had such company outward bound.
I went till there were no cottages found.
I turned and repented, but coming back
I saw no window but that was black.

Over the snow my creaking feet
Disturbed the slumbering village street
Like profanation, by your leave,
At ten o'clock of a winter eve.

26

The Wood-Pile

In December 1961, more than fifty years after Robert Frost wrote "The Wood-Pile," he used it as his Christmas card. He was eighty-seven years old, and it was still one of his favorites.

"The Wood-Pile" was first published in *North of Boston* in London in 1914. Exactly when he wrote it is uncertain. Frost said he had "largely written" it before he went to England, but he added the passage about the small bird when he was in England. One of the entries he made in his English notebook reads "As a bird flies before you and thinks it is pursued."

Frost did not identify a specific locale for the abandoned wood-pile of the poem. One scholar believes it originated in a passage in Nathaniel Hawthorne's American notebooks. But whether Frost found the wood-pile on one of the long walks he took into the neighboring countryside of the Derry farm, or whether it came from a book he was reading, the setting is vintage Frost New England—accurately rendered, without sentimental or pastoral enhancement. From its very first line, the scene is a bleak one: a desolate frozen swamp on a gray day. Even the encrusted snow underfoot cannot be trusted. Overcast days far outnumber sunny ones in New Hampshire and Vermont, and Frost knew well the leaden quiet of a cloudy winter day in the woods.

The wood-pile, part of everyday life for New England farmers, stands here as a man-made artifact in the midst of nature's unrelenting forces. Frost clearly knew all about wood-piles—their dimensions, how they were held together, and the coloring of the cord of maple after long exposure to the elements. He also knew that clematis, an indigenous vine belonging to the buttercup family, would wind itself around a deserted wood-pile "like a bundle."

Frost could identify with the woodcutter who wielded the ax that cut the firewood. It was the kind of hard work Frost had "spent himself" on during his decade as a Yankee farmer. He once called "chopping with an ax" one of his favorite kinds of labor; but "writing with a pen" was another, and from the beginning he preferred the pen over the ax.

Frost never said he was thinking of himself when he wrote this poem about a man who worked hard, then "turning to fresh tasks," left his "handiwork" behind. A biographical reading is intriguing, however. He wrote the final draft of it in England, soon after he left his life as a chicken farmer in New Hampshire behind him. As soon as the terms of his grandfather's will transferred ownership of the Derry farm to him, Frost sold it and used the proceeds to finance his move to England, where he could pursue his career as a poet. Like the woodcutter in the poem, he too turned "to fresh tasks" and did not look back.

Of course, the poem is about much more than Frost's decision to change careers. Frost himself attested to its deeper meanings when he called it one of his "parable" poems, adding "There are intimations in that, you know, hints." The hints have led many readers to view the poem as a statement about the deep division between humanity and nature, with nature moving on inexorably toward decay, oblivious to human considerations.

Frost gave us a few more hints about this poem when he proposed two questions about it: "Do you find any threat in The Wood Pile?" and "What is the quality of such a line as 'Like one who takes everything said as personal to himself?'" The bird passage from which the line is taken has subsequently received attention as a displacement of paranoia brought on by loneliness and fear.

But the line of the poem that has generated the biggest response is its final line, generally conceded to be one of Frost's most compelling images. Frost revealed a mundane source for the phrase "slow smokeless burning"—a magazine ad for a firearms firm describing an "Infallible Smokeless" powder. It was, Frost said, "one of my lucky snatches from an advertising page in the *Literary Digest* . . . one of those things a writer picks up by chance and steals them to new uses." The use he put the words to was sufficiently original to warrant high critical praise. A British review of *North of Boston* that appeared shortly after its publication set the tone for the host of positive assessments that have followed: "Poetry burns up out of it—as when a faint wind breathes upon smouldering embers. The simplest of Mr. Frost's poems—"The Wood-Pile"—had this clear strangeness throughout, and in its last line the magic of intensest insight."

The Wood-Pile

OUT walking in the frozen swamp one grey day
I paused and said, "I will turn back from here.
No, I will go on farther—and we shall see."
The hard snow held me, save where now and then
One foot went down. The view was all in lines
Straight up and down of tall slim trees
Too much alike to mark or name a place by
So as to say for certain I was here
Or somewhere else: I was just far from home.
A small bird flew before me. He was careful
To put a tree between us when he lighted,
And say no word to tell me who he was
Who was so foolish as to think what he thought.
He thought that I was after him for a feather —
The white one in his tail; like one who takes
Everything said as personal to himself.
One flight out sideways would have undeceived him.
And then there was a pile of wood for which
I forgot him and let his little fear
Carry him off the way I might have gone,
Without so much as wishing him good-night.
He went behind it to make his last stand.
It was a cord of maple, cut and split
And piled—and measured, four by four by eight.
And not another like it could I see.
No runner tracks in this year's snow looped near it.
And it was older sure than this year's cutting,
Or even last year's or the year's before.
The wood was grey and the bark warping off it
And the pile somewhat sunken. Clematis

Had wound strings round and round it like a bundle.
What held it though on one side was a tree
Still growing, and on one a stake and prop,
These latter about to fall. I thought that only
Someone who lived in turning to fresh tasks
Could so forget his handiwork on which
He spent himself, the labour of his axe,
And leave it there far from a useful fireplace
To warm the frozen swamp as best it could
With the slow smokeless burning of decay.

27

Mending Wall

"I wrote the poem 'Mending Wall' thinking of the old wall that I hadn't mended in several years and which must be in a terrible condition. I wrote that poem in England when I was very homesick for my old wall in New England." This recollection by Robert Frost in 1936 establishes the winter of 1913-14 in Beaconsfield, England, as the time and place he wrote the poem that many consider to be his signature piece.

A trip the Frost family took to Scotland from Beaconsfield in late August 1913 may have triggered his memory of the Derry farm stone wall. For Frost, "the best" part of the vacation in Scotland "was the time in Kingsbarns," where he saw some striking "dry stone dykes" on the long walks he took along the Firth of Fay. According to J. C. Smith, who often accompanied him, the stone dykes set Frost thinking about his stone wall back home in New Hampshire and provided the impetus for the poem.

The "old wall" he wrote about in the poem marked the boundary between his farm in Derry and that of his neighbor to the south, the French-Canadian Napoleon Guay. The line about the neighbor being all pine fits the description of Guay's property as recorded by Frost's daughter Lesley in the journal she kept as part of her home-school assignments. One passage describes a walk she and her father took along Mr. Guay's pine woods. The Guays were the Frosts' closest neighbors, and Mr. Guay helped Frost out repeatedly during the ten years they shared a property line. In 1903 Guay took care of their livestock for a month while the family took a trip to New York City. In 1907 he took over the farm chores when Frost was recuperating from a near-fatal bout with pneumonia. Guay was, in every sense, the "good neighbor" of the poem.

It is highly unlikely, however, that Guay ever said "Good fences make good neighbors." The phrase is proverbial and can be found in farmers' almanacs dating back to 1850. The passage about the damage inflicted by hunters does directly reflect the Derry farm. According to

Lesley: "On the way over to the big grove, we found the stone wall knocked down, in two places, and Carol found a shotgun shell."

Two of the key images in the poem—elves and a spell—can be traced to a story Frost wrote for his children during the Derry years. "The Last Apple Fall" opens with the admonition: "Fairies live in juniper bushes—you have to believe that" and goes on to chronicle the adventures of Lesley and Carol in the orchard:

> Their backs were to the wall so that when a stone fell off it they were taken by surprise. They hardly turned in time to see two little heads pop out of sight on the pasture side. Carol saw them better than Lesley. "Fairies!" he cried. Lesley said, "I can't believe it." "Fairies sure," said Carol.

Occasionally readers have assumed that the narrator is speaking for Frost, but the poet himself suggested "Maybe I was both fellows in the poem." He said he meant for there to be "no rigid separation between right and wrong. 'Mending Wall' simply contrasts two types of people." He maintained that he "played exactly fair in it. Twice I say 'Good fences' and twice 'Something there is—.'" Another time he claimed: "I am both wall-builder and wall-destroyer." Once, however, when asked "Wouldn't you like to get rid of walls?" he replied: "No, we always have walls—have always had them. While some are being torn down, others are being built up. Whether you want 'em or not you'll always have 'em."

In 1962, at the age of eighty-eight, he recited "Mending Wall" in Moscow. The Cold War with Russia was in high gear, and Frost's metaphorical wall had obvious parallels to the Berlin wall put up by Communist East Germany the year before. His trip climaxed with a ninety-minute one-on-one conversation with Premier Khrushchev, a meeting cited by the White House as instrumental in reducing tensions "on both sides of the Iron Curtain." It was just a few months before his death.

In the last year of Robert Frost's life, this distinctly regional poem had gone beyond its local roots and assumed global significance. The simple, metaphorically rich image that unifies the poem balances two diametrically opposed positions and points the way toward conflict resolutions of all kind.

Mending Wall

Something there is that doesn't love a wall,
That sends the frozen-ground-swell under it,
And spills the upper boulders in the sun;
And makes gaps even two can pass abreast.
The work of hunters is another thing:
I have come after them and made repair
Where they have left not one stone on a stone,
But they would have the rabbit out of hiding,
To please the yelping dogs. The gaps I mean,
No one has seen them made or heard them made,
But at spring mending-time we find them there.
I let my neighbor know beyond the hill;
And on a day we meet to walk the line
And set the wall between us once again.
We keep the wall between us as we go.
To each the boulders that have fallen to each.
And some are loaves and some so nearly balls
We have to use a spell to make them balance:
"Stay where you are until our backs are turned!"
We wear our fingers rough with handling them.
Oh, just another kind of outdoor game,
One on a side. It comes to little more:
There where it is we do not need the wall:
He is all pine and I am apple orchard.
My apple trees will never get across
And eat the cones under his pines, I tell him.
He only says, "Good fences make good neighbors."
Spring is the mischief in me, and I wonder
If I could put a notion in his head:
"Why do they make good neighbors? Isn't it

Where there are cows? But here there are no cows.
Before I built a wall I'd ask to know
What I was walling in or walling out,
And to whom I was like to give offense.
Something there is that doesn't love a wall,
That wants it down." I could say "Elves" to him,
But it's not elves exactly, and I'd rather
He said it for himself. I see him there
Bringing a stone grasped firmly by the top
In each hand, like an old-stone savage armed.
He moves in darkness as it seems to me,
Not of woods only and the shade of trees.
He will not go beyond his father's saying,
And he likes having thought of it so well
He says again, "Good fences make good neighbors."

28

After Apple-Picking

"After Apple-Picking" has been hailed as "one of the great triumphs of twentieth-century verse." Depending on who is doing the reading, it is about work, aspirations, failure, original sin, life's accomplishments and disappointments, getting old and getting tired, sleeping, dreaming, dying, and writing poetry. The diverse interpretations are all rooted in a simple metaphor—picking apples, which Frost recreates complete with the sight, sound, smell, and feel of the experience. The imagery is remarkable. The scent of apples, their color, the rumbling sound as they fill the cellar bin, the swaying of the ladder, the pressure of its rung on the instep arch—all are vividly evoked. Frost was aware of how well the images worked in this poem. In an inscription following "After Apple-Picking" in a copy of *Selected Poems*, he wrote: "Imagery and after-imagery are all there is to poetry."

Although Frost wrote this poem in Beaconsfield, England, in the fall of 1913, its subject and locale were prompted by the intense homesickness he was feeling for the New England he had left behind. Back in the fall of 1900, one of the deciding factors of the Frosts' move to Derry was their delight in the house and land that made up "the Magoon place" where they would be living. They were especially pleased with the two young apple trees that flanked the approach to the house and the good-sized apple orchard to the north. During the first year-and-a-half on the Derry farm, the fruit trees were the responsibility of Carl Burell, an old friend and former classmate who moved in with them as a helper. Carl was an experienced farmer, and he made a comfortable profit from the apples he harvested in exchange for his work. When Carl left, the orchard duties fell to Frost, who already had his hands full keeping up with the other chores. By 1906 he realized he would have to seek a teaching job to supplement the meager income he was able to earn from the farm. His days as a full-time farmer were over. The hyperbole in the poem of the "ten thousand thousand fruit to touch,/ Cherish in hand, lift down, and not let fall" could well be an expression of how he remembered the overwhelming work he faced as the "overtired" apple picker, disenchanted with the "great harvest" he had himself "desired" and overtaken by exhaustion.

Such an autobiographical interpretation is strengthened by Frost's own comments. During an evening of informal poetry reading in 1915, he told his friend Sidney Cox that "After Apple-Picking" had "the intoxication of extreme exhaustion" in it. At a more formal reading in 1958, he called it one of his "observing" poems. Sometimes, he said, "I am too observing . . . I've always been afraid of my own observations," particularly when "observing psychologically . . . seeing into people." This time he may have been seeing into himself. If read allegorically as a poem about one's life work, the apples can be equated with his poems, making it doubly revealing since at this point in his career, his success as a poet had been minimal.

The reference to the woodchuck and his long sleep in the concluding lines of the poem has confused many readers. Frost probably found the idea of comparing humans to woodchucks in Emerson's essay "Nature," where readers are told: "let us be men instead of woodchucks." A discussion of hibernation in another Emerson essay, "Fate," may have been the source for the term "the long sleep." In terms of the dream-ridden and exhausted state of the speaker in Frost's poem, he could be seeking the dreamless sleep of an animal or the months-long sleep of hibernation. Or a subtle hint of death and resurrection may also be implied.

Rueben Brower dismisses the poem's ending as one of "amused confusion," in tune with the "dreamy confusion of rhythm" that leads up to it. In a tour-de-force analysis of meter and rhyme, Brower details the "incantatory repetitions" in the "curious chain-like sentences, rich in end-rhymes and echoes." He calls it "the most beautiful example of freedom in rhyme and of freedom perfectly controlled."

In "After Apple-Picking" Frost creates a dreamscape that transcends its homey, pastoral roots. The tangible realities of an autumnal harvest on an apple farm in New Hampshire—a ladder "sticking through a tree"; an empty barrel; a sheet of ice from the drinking trough; the hibernating woodchuck—all become part of a "dream vision" that blurs the distinction between sleeping and waking, between fact and imagination, and gets the reader thinking about human goals, on earth and beyond. It is, another reader proclaims, one of Frost's "very great poems."

After Apple-Picking

My long two-pointed ladder's sticking through a tree
Toward heaven still,
And there's a barrel that I didn't fill
Beside it, and there may be two or three
Apples I didn't pick upon some bough.
But I am done with apple-picking now.
Essence of winter sleep is on the night,
The scent of apples: I am drowsing off.
I cannot rub the strangeness from my sight
I got from looking through a pane of glass
I skimmed this morning from the drinking trough
And held against the world of hoary grass.
It melted, and I let it fall and break.
But I was well
Upon my way to sleep before it fell,
And I could tell
What form my dreaming was about to take.
Magnified apples appear and disappear,
Stem end and blossom end,
And every fleck of russet showing clear.
My instep arch not only keeps the ache,
It keeps the pressure of a ladder-round.
I feel the ladder sway as the boughs bend.
And I keep hearing from the cellar bin
The rumbling sound
Of load on load of apples coming in.
For I have had too much
Of apple-picking: I am overtired
Of the great harvest I myself desired.
There were ten thousand thousand fruit to touch,

Cherish in hand, lift down, and not let fall.
For all
That struck the earth,
No matter if not bruised or spiked with stubble,
Went surely to the cider-apple heap
As of no worth.
One can see what will trouble
This sleep of mine, whatever sleep it is.
Were he not gone,
The woodchuck could say whether it's like his
Long sleep, as I describe its coming on,
Or just some human sleep.

29

Birches

It was Charley Peabody in Salem Depot, New Hampshire, who first taught Robert Frost how to swing birches. Both boys were twelve years old in 1886 when Rob's bold and fearless new "best friend" showed him how to climb a birch tree and ride it down to the ground. According to his daughter Lesley, Frost was still enjoying the sport in 1905, when he was twenty-seven and she was six. In the journal she kept as a child on the Derry farm, she wrote: "papa likes to swing" [birches better than I do.]

Frost captured the experience in the poem he originally called "Swinging Birches." He wrote it in 1913 in Beaconsfield, England, originally claiming to have written it "with one stroke of the pen." He later admitted, "'Birches' is two fragments soldered together so long ago I have forgotten where the joint is." The earlier draft was probably a fragment about birches and icicles that he wrote in 1906.

Frost's enthusiasm for this boyhood pastime is reflected in the poem. He remembers exactly how he flung himself down, feet first, kicking his way to the ground. Once, during one of his poetry reading trips, a group of young people were showing off for him by swinging "birches, straight up . . . when they got to the top, they threw themselves forward and got down to the ground head first." He was quick to point out: "We didn't do it that way." On another occasion, a woman refused to attend his reading because "she wouldn't come to listen to a person who could tell such a story about a birch tree. She had one in her yard and she knew very well it would break if anyone did do a thing like that." She concluded, Frost said, "that I didn't know what I was talking about." He subsequently acknowledged to another audience: "It was almost sacrilegious climbing a birch tree till it bent, till it gave and swooped to the ground. But that's what boys did in those days."

On Lesley Frost's first try, she climbed up a "hi birch and came down with it, " stopping in the air about three feet from the ground, when her "papa" caught her. "At first I was scared," she wrote. Frost too had been somewhat timid at first, but he eventually followed his more adventurous young friend's lead. Retrospectively Frost shed some light on how he felt, although he broadened the scope to include a lot more than the danger in swinging birches: he observed "there are no two things as important in life and art as being threatened and being saved. . . . All our ingenuity is lavished on getting into danger legitimately so that we may be genuinely rescued."

But the poem is more about striking a balance between getting "away from earth" and then coming "back to it" than it is about overcoming fear. He told his former student, John Bartlett: "It isn't in man's nature to live an isolated life. Freedom isn't to be had that way. Going away and looking at man in perspective, and then coming back . . . that is what's sane and good." In one interview in 1931, he extolled the virtues of "striving to get the balance." He added, "I should expect life to be back and forward—now more individual on the farm, now more social in the city," reflecting the pattern of his own life. "Earth's the right place for love," he says in the poem, and for him that meant love and communion with his fellow human beings. As he got older, another line came to mean the most to him: "It's when I'm weary of considerations."

The two opening lines paint a familiar New England sight—leaning birches. In the icicle passage that follows, Frost adds auditory and tactile imagery to his visual rendering: the trees "click," the breeze rises, the sun warms, the icicles shatter and avalanche. The image that captivated Frost's own imagination most is the comparison of birches to girls kneeling down with their hair thrown before them to dry in the sun. Fifteen years after he wrote that simile, he was still using it to describe a grove of white paper birches on the new farm he had purchased in South Shaftsbury, Vermont, in 1928. He called them his "lady trees" and liked to take long walks out their way to "keep faith" with them.

This is one of Frost's most anthologized poems. Its meter and language make it accessible and popular. By combining the rhythm of the speaking voice with the idiom of the Yankee vernacular, Frost skillfully creates the fiction of everyday talk, providing a comfort zone for newcomers to poetry. Yet the poem has a lyrical and metaphorical quality that belies its down-home surface appearance, and the poem's lines and images stay with the reader as no casual conversation ever does.

Birches

When I see birches bend to left and right
Across the lines of straighter darker trees,
I like to think some boy's been swinging them.
But swinging doesn't bend them down to stay.
Ice-storms do that. Often you must have seen them
Loaded with ice a sunny winter morning
After a rain. They click upon themselves
As the breeze rises, and turn many-colored
As the stir cracks and crazes their enamel.
Soon the sun's warmth makes them shed crystal shells
Shattering and avalanching on the snow-crust —
Such heaps of broken glass to sweep away
You'd think the inner dome of heaven had fallen.
They are dragged to the withered bracken by the load,
And they seem not to break; though once they are bowed
So low for long, they never right themselves:
You may see their trunks arching in the woods
Years afterwards, trailing their leaves on the ground
Like girls on hands and knees that throw their hair
Before them over their heads to dry in the sun.
But I was going to say when Truth broke in
With all her matter-of-fact about the ice-storm
(Now I am free to be poetical?)
I should prefer to have some boy bend them
As he went out and in to fetch the cows—
Some boy too far from town to learn baseball,
Whose only play was what he found himself,
Summer or winter, and could play alone.
One by one he subdued his father's trees
By riding them down over and over again

Until he took the stiffness out of them,
And not one but hung limp, not one was left
For him to conquer. He learned all there was
To learn about not launching out too soon
And so not carrying the tree away
Clear to the ground. He always kept his poise
To the top branches, climbing carefully
With the same pains you use to fill a cup
Up to the brim, and even above the brim.
Then he flung outward, feet first, with a swish,
Kicking his way down through the air to the ground.
So was I once myself a swinger of birches.
And so I dream of going back to be.
It's when I'm weary of considerations,
And life is too much like a pathless wood
Where your face burns and tickles with the cobwebs
Broken across it, and one eye is weeping
From a twig's having lashed across it open.
I'd like to get away from earth awhile
And then come back to it and begin over.
May no fate willfully misunderstand me
And half grant what I wish and snatch me away
Not to return. Earth's the right place for love:
I don't know where it's likely to go better.
I'd like to go by climbing a birch tree,
And climb black branches up a snow-white trunk
Toward heaven, till the tree could bear no more,
But dipped its top and set me down again.
That would be good both going and coming back.
One could do worse than be a swinger of birches.

30

Home Burial

When Robert Frost wrote this poem during the winter of 1912-1913 in Beaconsfield, England, he knew all too well what it was like to grieve the death of a child. In 1900 his three-year-old son was stricken with a deadly form of cholera and died within a matter of days. Yet Frost insisted repeatedly that this poem was not about Elliott or about his and Elinor's response to his death.

It was inspired, he said, by the premature death of another child whose parents separated as a result of the grief that followed. Elinor's older sister Leona and her husband Nathaniel Harvey lost their first-born child in 1895. Frost spent that summer in Ossipee Mountain Park in New Hampshire because of the domestic dispute that followed the child's death. Leona left her husband and accepted a commission to paint portraits in the area, Elinor accompanied her, and Frost went along to be with Elinor. (The Harveys later reconciled and subsequently had three more children.)

In spite of the connection Frost made with the Harveys' situation, and his denials that the poem was autobiographical, the personal parallels are difficult to dismiss. Although Elliott's death devastated both him and Elinor, the ways in which their grief affected them and their return to daily life differed as drastically as those expressed by the couple in the poem, and along the same male/female lines. Frost's response is stated in a letter he wrote to his friend, Louis Untermeyer: "And I suppose I am a brute in that my nature refuses to carry sympathy to the point . . . of dying just because someone else dies." In a letter to another friend, J. J. Lankes, he revealed how differently Elinor reacted: "I refused to be bowed down as much as she was by other deaths." In commenting on "Home Burial," Frost credited the husband with being "more practical and matter-of-fact about death than the woman." But the most convincing echo from Frost's real-life tragedy is his use of the phrase "the world's evil." The wife in the poem issues this blanket condemnation using exactly the same words Elinor did over and over again after Elliott's death. In an attempt to explain the factual sources of his poetry, Frost said, "Some of the poems combine many incidents, many people and places, but all are real." "Home Burial" appears to be one of these.

Although Frost did not include the poem in his readings (it was "too sad," he said, for him to read aloud in public), he did not hesitate to point out some of the things he liked about it. He thought the husband's words "'If—you—do'" were "sufficiently self-expressive." He prided himself on his use of "oh" in the phrase "'Oh,' and again, 'Oh,'" conveying the wide variety of emotions the word was capable of expressing. He was proudest of all of the wife's exclamation: "'Don't, don't, don't, don't.'" He told Sidney Cox that "the four 'don'ts' were the supreme thing in it," and he told John Cournos that while the effect of the four repetitions would be good in prose, it "gained something from the way they are placed in the verse." The poet Amy Lowell agreed with Frost. In her review, she singles out the "Don't" line for high praise: "that cry of the woman is terrible in its stark truth. Printed words can go no further than this."

"Home Burial" was published in *North of Boston* in 1914. When Frost was looking for a title for this second book, he considered calling it *New England Eclogues.* That title would have acknowledged his debt to the Latin poet Virgil. It was Virgil who perfected the eclogue, a poem that celebrates country life and usually takes the form of a dialogue between two shepherds. In his poems of country life, Frost admitted he had deliberately "dropped to an everyday level of diction" in order to capture the speaking voice in the written word. He had first heard that voice, he said, "from a printed page in a Virgilian eclogue."

Frost's speaking-voice style is not a mechanical recording of the everyday speech of New Englanders. A close look will reveal a poet at work. The poem follows the formal meter of blank verse, which mandates five two-part beats to each line. Frost follows that rule, but he allows the speech rhythms to override the regular beat as the emotional tension increases. Another technique is alliteration, as in the "L" sound in the wife's line: "Leap up, like that, like that, and land so lightly."

"Home Burial" has been interpreted as being about the eternal battle between the sexes. Others have praised it for revealing "the heart of womanhood." To one reader, it is about "miscommunication." It is all of these. In it, with characteristic Frostian irony, words are used to show how inadequate words can be.

Home Burial

He saw her from the bottom of the stairs
Before she saw him. She was starting down,
Looking back over her shoulder at some fear.
She took a doubtful step and then undid it
To raise herself and look again. He spoke
Advancing toward her: "What is it you see
From up there always—for I want to know."
She turned and sank upon her skirts at that,
And her face changed from terrified to dull.
He said to gain time: "What is it you see,"
Mounting until she cowered under him.
"I will find out now—you must tell me, dear."
She, in her place, refused him any help
With the least stiffening of her neck and silence.
She let him look, sure that he wouldn't see,
Blind creature; and a while he didn't see.
But at last he murmured, "Oh," and again, "Oh."

"What is it—what?" she said.

                              "Just that I see."

"You don't," she challenged. "Tell me what it is."

"The wonder is I didn't see at once.
I never noticed it from here before.
I must be wonted to it—that's the reason.
The little graveyard where my people are!
So small the window frames the whole of it.
Not so much larger than a bedroom, is it?
There are three stones of slate and one of marble,
Broad-shouldered little slabs there in the sunlight

On the sidehill. We haven't to mind those.
But I understand: it is not the stones,
But the child's mound——"

"Don't, don't, don't, don't," she cried.

She withdrew shrinking from beneath his arm
That rested on the banister, and slid downstairs;
And turned on him with such a daunting look,
He said twice over before he knew himself:
"Can't a man speak of his own child he's lost?"

"Not you! Oh, where's my hat? Oh, I don't need it!
I must get out of here. I must get air.
I don't know rightly whether any man can."

"Amy! Don't go to someone else this time.
Listen to me. I won't come down the stairs."
He sat and fixed his chin between his fists.
"There's something I should like to ask you, dear."

"You don't know how to ask it"

                                    "Help me, then."
Her fingers moved the latch for all reply.

"My words are nearly always an offence.
I don't know how to speak of anything
So as to please you. But I might be taught,
I should suppose. I can't say I see how.
A man must partly give up being a man
With woman-folk. We could have some arrangement
By which I'd bind myelf to keep hands off
Anything special you're a-mind to name.
Though I don't like such things 'twixt those that love.
Two that don't love can't live together without them.

But two that do can't live together with them."
She moved the latch a little. "Don't—don't go.
Don't carry it to someone else this time.
Tell me about it if it's something human.
Let me into your grief. I'm not so much
Unlike other folks as your standing there
Apart would make me out. Give me my chance.
I do think, though, you overdo it a little.
What was it brought you up to think it the thing
To take your mother-loss of a first child
So inconsolably—in the face of love.
You'd think his memory might be satisfied——"

"There you go sneering now!"

                    "I'm not, I'm not!
You make me angry. I'll come down to you.
God, what a woman! And it's come to this,
A man can't speak of his own child that's dead."

"You can't because you don't know how.
If you had any feelings, you that dug
With your own hand—how could you?—his little grave;
I saw you from that very window there,
Making the gravel leap and leap in air,
Leap up, like that, like that, and land so lightly
And roll back down the mound beside the hole.
I thought, Who is that man? I didn't know you.
And I crept down the stairs and up the stairs
To look again, and still your spade kept lifting.
Then you came in. I heard your rumbling voice
Out in the kitchen, and I don't know why,
But I went near to see with my own eyes.
You could sit there with the stains on your shoes
Of the fresh earth from your own baby's grave

And talk about your everyday concerns.
You had stood the spade up against the wall
Outside there in the entry, for I saw it."

"I shall laugh the worst laugh I ever laughed.
I'm cursed. God, if I don't believe I'm cursed."

"I can repeat the very words you were saying.
'Three foggy mornings and one rainy day
Will rot the best birch fence a man can build.'
Think of it, talk like that at such a time!
What had how long it takes a birch to rot
To do with what was in the darkened parlour?
You couldn't care! The nearest friends can go
With anyone to death, comes so far short
They might as well not try to go at all.
No, from the time when one is sick to death,
One is alone, and he dies more alone.
Friends make pretence of following to the grave,
But before one is in it, their minds are turned
And making the best of their way back to life
And living people, and things they understand.
But the world's evil. I won't have grief so
If I can change it. Oh, I won't, I won't."

"There, you have said it all and you feel better.
You won't go now. You're crying. Close the door.
The heart's gone out of it: why keep it up?
Amy! There's someone coming down the road!"

"You—oh, you think the talk is all. I must go —
Somewhere out of this house. How can I make you——"

"If—you—do!" She was opening the door wider.
"Where do you mean to go? First tell me that.
I'll follow and bring you back by force. I *will!*—"

31

The Cow in Apple Time

A drunken cow is not the usual stuff of poetry, but Robert Frost's self-confessed "innate mischievousness" was at work when he wrote this poem in 1914. He was in England, but he was thinking about a belligerent cow he once owned back in New Hampshire. Like the cow in the poem, the cow in Derry was "the only cow" on the farm, one given to running away. His daughter Lesley's journal records five occasions in 1905 alone when her father had to chase after the rambunctious cow. In the poem, the cow bellows from "a knoll against the sky," a backdrop that fits the contour of the hill on the Guay property adjoining the Derry farm.

The poem has an English source as well. Frost said he had "the giant animals on the . . . Prince Albert Memorial in London" in mind when he wrote the poem. Frost undoubtedly saw the Memorial during the family's initial explorations of London, but he would have been able to revisit it in April and May 1914, when the Frosts lived in rented rooms not far from Hyde Park. The connection in the poet's mind between the huge bronze sculpture and the "heroic-sized" but humble cow, reeling from the effect of fermented windfall apples, prompted Frost to write a mock-heroic poem, even to the use of traditional heroic couplets.

He thought it was one of his "cruder" poems, but readers have responded differently, calling it "frankly humorous," "delightful," and "delicious." Louis Untermeyer, his friend and anthologizer, pointed out that "some have read astonishing things into it." None more so than Lawrance Thompson, who deemed it to be "a puritanical farm fable . . . a figurative portrait of a young married woman who runs away from home and suffers the consequences of a sinfully rebellious life." Since this interpretation was not published until three years after Frost's death, Frost was spared the embarrassment of seeing what his official biographer had to say about the poem he had written in fun.

The Cow in Apple Time

Something inspires the only cow of late
To make no more of a wall than an open gate,
And think no more of wall-builders than fools.
Her face is flecked with pomace and she drools
A cider syrup. Having tasted fruit,
She scorns a pasture withering to the root.
She runs from tree to tree where lie and sweeten
The windfalls spiked with stubble and worm-eaten.
She leaves them bitten when she has to fly.
She bellows on a knoll against the sky.
Her udder shrivels and the milk goes dry.

32

The Sound of the Trees

After his return to New Hampshire from his three-year stay in England, Robert Frost declared, "I never saw New England as clearly as when I was in Old England." "The Sound of the Trees," written in Ryton, near Dymock in Gloucestershire, England, in 1914, is a case in point. The cottage where Frost and his family lived that fall was surrounded by the English countryside, and Frost admitted that he was writing under the influence of the English poet, Lascelles Abercrombie, who had invited the Frosts to share living quarters with him and his family. Nevertheless, Frost insisted that he was thinking of a group of trees near his old home in New England when he wrote this poem.

Trees are everywhere in New England, and their presence is equally omnipresent in Frost's poetry. Often he creates images of the woods as a place of rest and retreat, as in one of his best known poems, "Stopping by Woods on a Snowy Evening." In "The Sound of the Trees," however, the imagery is disturbing, not inviting. In a list of questions Frost prepared in response to an inquiry about how to read his poetry, Frost wrote: "Do you find any threat in The Sound of Trees?" Clearly he was implying that a threat—and a corresponding fear—is there.

The fear is largely undefined, making it all the more difficult to interpret. Paradoxes abound. "We suffer" the trees' noise, yet the speaker identifies with them, swaying as he watches them sway. The trees are rooted and cannot move, yet "they are that that talks of going." And although their "voice" may scare him into running away, the final "I shall be gone" seems to have a note of elation in it. The simultaneous feelings of exhilaration and fright may seem paradoxical, but they fit the emotions of someone wanting to set out for the unknown. Jay Parini believes this theme is a strong element in the poem, similar to that found in "Birches."

Another reviewer, Robert McPhillips, concludes that "The Sound of the Trees" was used as a deliberate foil to "The Road Not Taken." They are the only poems printed in italics in *Mountain Interval*, and they serve as the boundaries of the book, with "The Road Not Taken" on the opening page and "The Sound of the Trees" on the last. Both poems are about making choices—the balanced, measured perspective first, contrasted by the more "reckless" decision contemplated at the end.

The Sound of the Trees

I wonder about the trees.
Why do we wish to bear
Forever the noise of these
More than another noise
So close to our dwelling place?
We suffer them by the day
Till we lose all measure of pace,
And fixity in our joys,
And acquire a listening air.
They are that that talks of going
But never gets away;
And that talks no less for knowing,
As it grows wiser and older,
That now it means to stay.
My feet tug at the floor
And my head sways to my shoulder
Sometimes when I watch trees sway,
From the window or the door.
I shall set forth for somewhere,
I shall make the reckless choice
Some day when they are in voice
And tossing so as to scare
The white clouds over them on.
I shall have less to say,
But I shall be gone.

33

The Exposed Nest

This poem was written in Franconia, New Hampshire, in 1915 after Robert Frost returned from England. Frost later contradicted himself, saying he had written it two years earlier, but there is no confusion about the event dramatized in the poem; it occurred during the years Frost and his family lived on the Derry farm.

Frost offers us a refreshing glimpse of his wife Elinor in a playful mood in contrast to the more sombre figure portrayed in a poem like "My November Guest." A togetherness of spirit and purpose marks the couple in "The Exposed Nest." Initially the speaker is ready to join what he thinks is a "make-believe" game. Then he becomes a helpmate in his companion's mission to protect the baby birds. They share as well in the poem's final reprimand, when he asks her, almost hopefully, if she remembers whatever happened to the birds they tried to save. Frost's portrayal of the incident gives us a sense of the everyday intimacy he and Elinor shared when they were simply a farmer and his wife on a New Hampshire farm.

It is this simplicity—and the authenticity with which Frost conveys it—that keeps his poetry about such potentially sentimental subjects as saving baby birds from becoming saccharine. William Pritchard points out that Frost "can be beautifully protective . . . of his New England material." In Pritchard's discussion of this poem, he conjectures what "a less subtle writer" might have done with the material: "We might observe love strengthened between the two people because of their act of caring; or we might have baby birds and mother reunited in a benign stroke of fortune." But Frost chooses to give us a more realistic story without the popular happy ending. It is an example, in Pritchard's words, of Frost's "unwillingness to exploit nature" in order to manipulate his readers.

Nature is an integral part of Frost's poetry, enriching his imagery with sharp observations and concrete details, but he is more of a people poet than a nature poet. Frost's concern is with how people and nature interact. More often than not, they are at cross purposes. While Frost was at Harvard, he studied with American philosopher Josiah Royce, whose lectures on evolution focused on reconciling idealism with the realities of natural science. Several of Frost's poems grapple with the same paradoxes.

In this poem, it is a man-made machine that destroys the nest's protective cover, and the couple's "meddling" may not have helped the birds after all. Nature does not concern itself with human problems. And humans, in their own struggle for survival, do not always concern themselves with nature's welfare. The woman and her partner's involvement may have been well intentioned, but it was short-lived.

In the speaker's blunt, but honest explanation—"We turned to other things"—Frost echoes a poem he wrote a year earlier and foreshadows one he will write the following year. In "Home Burial" (1914), the father turns to other everyday matters to overcome his grief. And in "Out, Out——" (1916), Frost writes: "And they, since they / Were not the one dead, turned to their affairs." Such stoicism is not a denial of caring. Rather it is a confirmation of life. To survive the hardships of living on a New England farm in the early twentieth-century, one needed endurance, fortitude, and hard work. There was no room for self-indulgent regrets over what is lost, even though the speaker cannot help wondering if any of the fledglings learned "to use their wings."

The Exposed Nest

You were forever finding some new play.
So when I saw you down on hands and knees
In the meadow, busy with the new-cut hay,
Trying, I thought, to set it up on end,
I went to show you how to make it stay,
If that was your idea, against the breeze,
And, if you asked me, even help pretend
To make it root again and grow afresh.
But 'twas no make-believe with you to-day,
Nor was the grass itself your real concern,
Though I found your hand full of wilted fern,
Steel-bright June-grass, and blackening heads of clover.
'Twas a nest full of young birds on the ground
The cutter-bar had just gone champing over
(Miraculously without tasting flesh)
And left defenseless to the heat and light.
You wanted to restore them to their right
Of something interposed between their sight
And too much world at once—could means be found.
The way the nest-full every time we stirred
Stood up to us as to a mother-bird
Whose coming home has been too long deferred,
Made me ask would the mother-bird return
And care for them in such a change of scene
And might our meddling make her more afraid.
That was a thing we could not wait to learn.
We saw the risk we took in doing good,
But dared not spare to do the best we could
Though harm should come of it; so built the screen

You had begun, and gave them back their shade.
All this to prove we cared. Why is there then
No more to tell? We turned to other things.
I haven't any memory—have you?—
Of ever coming to the place again
To see if the birds lived the first night through,
And so at last to learn to use their wings.

34

The Road Not Taken

When poet laureate Robert Pinsky asked Americans to name their favorite poem, "The Road Not Taken" received the most votes. The survey's report, issued in April 2000, is based on 18,000 written, videotaped, and recorded responses. Ironically, America's most popular poem is also Robert Frost's most misunderstood. He meant it as a joke on a friend who could not make up his mind. But the friend did not see the satire in it—and neither do most readers, who usually take the poem to be a straightforward call to follow the road less traveled.

While Frost was in England, he became close friends with fellow writer Edward Thomas. They took long walks together in search of rare plants, Thomas leading the way through his native Gloucestershire countryside and inevitably agonizing over which path to follow. After one fruitful excursion, Frost said to him: "No matter which road you take, you'll always sigh, and wish you'd taken another."

Frost recalled that he wrote this poem "while I was sitting on a sofa in the middle of England" in 1914. He did not complete it, however, until the following year, after he returned to New Hampshire. Thomas's letters to Frost in 1915 were more indecisive than ever, struggling with the larger issue of whether Thomas should enlist in the war against Germany. Frost, hoping to put a lighter spin on his friend's vacillations, mailed a copy of the poem to him, but Thomas did not understand he was its target until Frost enlightened him.

The poem may fail as parody, but it succeeds in its rendition of the archetypal symbol of crossroads and the dilemma they pose. Frost's sensitivity to the image is revealed in a letter he wrote from Plymouth, New Hampshire, in 1912: "Two lonely cross-roads that themselves cross each other I have walked several times this winter without meeting or overtaking so much as a single person on foot or on runners. The practically unbroken condition of both for several days after a snow or a blow proves that neither is much travelled." Written six months before his departure to England, this observation establishes a New England source that predates his walking experiences with Thomas.

Frost warned his readers: "be careful . . . it's a tricky poem." He also told them: "You can go along over these rhymes just as if you didn't know that they were there." This was a poem "that talks past the rhymes," he said, and he took it as a compliment when his readers told him they could hear him talking in it.

The Road Not Taken

Two roads diverged in a yellow wood,
And sorry I could not travel both
And be one traveler, long I stood
And looked down one as far as I could
To where it bent in the undergrowth;

Then took the other, as just as fair,
And having perhaps the better claim,
Because it was grassy and wanted wear;
Though as for that the passing there
Had worn them really about the same,

And both that morning equally lay
In leaves no step had trodden black.
Oh, I kept the first for another day!
Yet knowing how way leads on to way,
I doubted if I should ever come back.

I shall be telling this with a sigh
Somewhere ages and ages hence:
Two roads diverged in a wood, and I —
I took the one less traveled by,
And that has made all the difference.

35

"Out, Out—"

Robert Frost felt this poem was "too cruel to read in public," and he seldom included it in his poetry readings. He knew the boy whose death inspired it. Raymond Fitzgerald was the son of Michael Fitzgerald, at whose hotel Frost spent his first summer in the White Mountains of New Hampshire in 1906. Raymond was one of the boys Frost and his children played games with during the next three summers, when the Frosts stayed at John and Margaret Lynch's nearby farm. It was there in 1910 that Frost heard about Raymond's accident.

He did not write "Out, Out—" until the summer of 1915, however. Frost had returned from his three years in England and was back in the Franconia area. He bought a farm outside the village of Sugar Hill, near the Lynches, with a view overlooking the five peaks of the Franconia Range. The panoramic setting may have reminded him of the Fitzgerald farm on nearby Garnet Hill. It overlooked five mountain ranges to the west toward Vermont, the same view described in the poem.

The March 31, 1910, edition of *The Littleton Courier* of Littleton, New Hampshire, carried the following story:

> Raymond Tracy Fitzgerald, one of the twin sons of Michael G. and Margaret Fitzgerald of Bethlehem, died at his home Thursday afternoon, March 24, as the result of an accident by which one of his hands was badly hurt in a sawing machine. The young man was assisting in sawing up some wood in his own dooryard with a saw-ing machine and accidentally hit the loose pulley, causing the saw to descend upon his hand, cutting and lacerating it badly. Raymond was taken into the house and a physician was immediately sum-moned, but he died very suddenly from the effects of the shock, which produced heart failure . . .

Frost's poetic rendering omits two explanations provided by the reporter. Instead of suggesting that the cause of the accident might have been the boy's carelessness, the poem proposes, even if only mo-mentarily, that the saw "Leaped out at the boy's hand," making the machine the culprit. The mechanized saw shatters the harmony of the natural environment (its snarling and rattling is repeated three times); it becomes a symbol of the industrialization encroaching on the old-fashioned Yankee way of doing things.

Instead of explaining the boy's death as a shock-induced heart attack, the poem attributes his death to the nature of the rural world in which he lives. According to John F. Lynen, any disruption of that "perfectly organized world" can lead to catastrophe, and the boy, responding "in a flash of intuition" understands that he cannot go on living without his hand. His misguided yet inevitable reaction heightens the tragedy. The Puritan work ethic comes into play too, since it is a mere "boy," "a child at heart" "Doing a man's work" who becomes the victim. When his sister calls him in to supper, heralding an end to the work, the saw strikes.

The two closing lines reflect another trait often associated with New England: a taciturn stoicism, unemotional in the face of a harrowing loss. Frost lost his own three-year-old son Elliott to cholera in 1900. Devastating as the death was to him, he believed the living needed to carry on with their lives. Reader response to the end of "'Out, Out—'" has varied. Some find it "uncomfortable," cold and stern, while others deem it "sincere," "natural," and necessary for survival in the face of economic realities. Radcliffe Squires admires its "deadly directness" and the way Frost holds together two "mutually accusing ideas": the need to have pity and the need to survive.

The title of the poem is taken from Macbeth's soliloquy after his wife's suicide that begins with "Out, out, brief candle!" and ends with a condemnation of life as "a tale / Told by an idiot, full of sound and fury, / Signifying nothing." The grim Shakespearean allusion deepens the irony of the poem by juxtaposing the murdering Macbeth and his pursuit of power with the fate of the nameless and blameless rural youth.

In a famous review of Hawthorne's short stories, Melville observed that contrary to first impressions, "Young Goodman Brown" was not a sunny tale about a "goody two-shoes" but was as dark and deep as Dante. Lionel Trilling, one of Frost's contemporaries, made a similar assessment of Frost's poetry. He refuted the generally accepted view of Frost as the poet of bucolic pastorals and called him "a terrifying poet." Nowhere is that more true than in "Out, Out —."

"Out, Out —"

The buzz-saw snarled and rattled in the yard
And made dust and dropped stove-length sticks of wood,
Sweet-scented stuff when the breeze drew across it.
And from there those that lifted eyes could count
Five mountain ranges one behind the other
Under the sunset far into Vermont.
And the saw snarled and rattled, snarled and rattled,
As it ran light, or had to bear a load.
And nothing happened: day was all but done.
Call it a day, I wish they might have said
To please the boy by giving him the half hour
That a boy counts so much when saved from work.
His sister stood beside them in her apron
To tell them "Supper." At that word, the saw,
As if to prove saws knew what supper meant,
Leaped out at the boy's hand, or seemed to leap—
He must have given the hand. However it was,
Neither refused the meeting. But the hand!
The boy's first outcry was a rueful laugh,
As he swung toward them holding up the hand
Half in appeal, but half as if to keep
The life from spilling. Then the boy saw all—
Since he was old enough to know, big boy
Doing a man's work, though a child at heart—
He saw all spoiled. "Don't let him cut my hand off—
The doctor, when he comes. Don't let him, sister!"
So. But the hand was gone already.
The doctor put him in the dark of ether.
He lay and puffed his lips out with his breath.

And then—the watcher at his pulse took fright.
No one believed. They listened at his heart.
Little—less—nothing!—and that ended it.
No more to build on there. And they, since they
Were not the one dead, turned to their affairs.

36

An Encounter

A conversation between a man and a telephone pole is the unlikely subject of "An Encounter." Robert Frost wrote it in 1916, but the incident and the setting date back to 1909, when he, Elinor, and the children spent the summer camping in northern Vermont near Lake Willoughby. Carl Burell recommended the area as ideal for botanical excursions. It turned out to be a hot and wet summer, full of "weather breeder" days that foretold torrents of rain. The poem gives an account of such a day in which the speaker finds himself face to face with an artifact of the industrialized civilization he had gone into the wilderness to escape.

Frost was skeptical, if not downright hostile, toward progress. He once berated himself for believing "even for the least division of an hour that there is any such thing as progress." He was ready to admit that he had seen enormous changes take place. In a letter to his grandson, William Prescott Frost, he wrote: "Electricity has come into use in my life time. When I came to New England in 1885, there wasn't a telephone in the city I lived in, Lawrence, Mass., and there wasn't an electric light."

But Frost had his doubts about the value of the changes. "Whatever progress may be taken to mean," he said, it didn't "mean making the world any easier a place in which to save your soul." On the other hand, withdrawing from the "improved" world of commerce and industry might help. For example, "bog trotting" in search of wild orchids had acquired an almost religious quality of awe and worship for Frost. In this poem a similar religious connection is suggested by the use of such words as "heaven," "a resurrected tree," and "raised again."

The theological implications are undercut, however, by the ironic tone and the comic effect of the exaggerated language. In the intentionally humorous confrontation between the seeker of rare orchids and the technological marvel of the telephone, the speaker claims the right to spend his time as aimlessly as he pleases, "half looking" for the Calypso Bulbosa, an orchid species that was virtually extinct in New England. Once again, Frost may have never been more serious than when he was fooling.

An Encounter

Once on the kind of day called "weather breeder,"
When the heat slowly hazes and the sun
By its own power seems to be undone,
I was half boring through, half climbing through
A swamp of cedar. Choked with oil of cedar
And scurf of plants, and weary and over-heated,
And sorry I ever left the road I knew,
I paused and rested on a sort of hook
That had me by the coat as good as seated,
And since there was no other way to look,
Looked up toward heaven, and there against the blue,
Stood over me a resurrected tree,
A tree that had been down and raised again —
A barkless spectre. He had halted too,
As if for fear of treading upon me.
I saw the strange position of his hands —
Up at his shoulders, dragging yellow strands
Of wire with something in it from men to men.
"You here?" I said. "Where aren't you nowadays
And what's the news you carry—if you know?
And tell me where you're off for—Montreal?
Me? I'm not off for anywhere at all.
Sometimes I wander out of beaten ways
Half looking for the orchid Calypso."

A Selective Chronology of Robert Frost's Life

1874   Born on March 26 in San Francisco, California, son of Isabelle Moodie and William Prescott Frost, Jr.

1885   Father dies of tuberculosis; moves with his mother and sister to grandfather's home in Lawrence, Massachusetts, then to Salem, New Hampshire.

1892   Graduates from Lawrence High School as co-valedictorian with Elinor White; enters Dartmouth College in fall, withdraws in December.

1895   Marries Elinor White.

1896   First child, Elliott, born.

1897   Enters Harvard University as special student.

1899   Withdraws from Harvard; daughter Lesley born.

1900   Elliott dies of cholera in July; moves to poultry farm in Derry, New Hampshire, in October; mother dies in November.

1902   Son Carol is born.

1903   Daughter Irma is born.

1905   Daughter Marjorie is born.

1906   Begins teaching at Pinkerton Academy in Derry.

1911   Accepts teaching position at State Normal School and moves family to Plymouth, New Hampshire; sells Derry farm in November.

1912   Sails to England with his family in August; rents a cottage in Beaconsfield.

1913   *A Boy's Will* published in London.

1914   Moves to Gloucestershire; *North of Boston* published in London.

1915	Returns to America; buys farm in Franconia, New Hampshire; begins life-long career as speaker and public reader of his poetry.
1916	*Mountain Interval* published in New York.
1917	Begins teaching at Amherst College in Massachusetts, an association that continues sporadically for the rest of his life.
1920	Buys farm in South Shaftsbury, Vermont, and moves into the Stone House.
1921	Appointed Poet in Residence at University of Michigan in Ann Arbor, where he serves for several terms, on and off, until 1926.
1924	Receives Pulitzer Prize for *New Hampshire*; first grandchild, William Prescott Frost, born.
1929	Buys and moves into the Gulley farm in South Shaftsbury, Vermont; participates in Bread Loaf Writers' Conference in Ripton, Vermont.
1931	Receives Pulitzer Prize for *Collected Poems*.
1937	Receives Pulitzer Prize for *A Further Range*.
1938	Elinor dies in Gainesville, Florida, in March; Frost returns to Bread Loaf Writers' Conference in summer; Kathleen Morrison becomes his secretary, a role she will keep until his death.
1940	Buys Homer Noble Farm in Ripton, Vermont; moves into a cabin on the farm for the summer.
1941	Buys and moves into the house at 35 Brewster Street, Cambridge, Massachusetts, which will become his primary residence with summers in Ripton and winters in South Miami, Florida.
1943	Receives his fourth Pulitzer Prize for *A Witness Tree*; continues to write, publish, receive honors and awards, and maintain a full schedule of poetry readings for two more decades.
1961	Reads his poetry at John F. Kennedy's presidential inauguration; named Poet Laureate of Vermont.
1962	Gives poetry readings in Leningrad and Moscow as part of a cultural exchange program with Russia, meets with Khruschev.
1963	Dies January 29 at Peter Bent Brigham Hospital in Boston; public memorial service at Amherst College; ashes interred in the Frost family plot in Old Bennington, Vermont.

How to Start a Frost Poetry Circle

If you have enjoyed browsing through this book, you can increase the pleasure you have found in reading Robert Frost's poems by sharing your responses to the poetry with others. The best way to do this is to start a Frost Poetry Circle. It's easy to do, rewarding, and fun.

Find some soul mates.

All you need to begin are three or four other like-minded individuals who are drawn to Frost's poetry. Larger groups will work, but in this case, bigger is not better. A small group will encourage participation and help keep the discussion friendly and informal.

Recruiting others to join you can be as easy as making a few telephone calls. Contact friends or acquaintances you think might enjoy exploring the comfortable but intriguing world of Frost's poetry. Remind them that if they can read the poetry (almost everyone has read some Frost poems in the course of a lifetime), they can talk about what the poem means to them. You can quote Frost on it. He was notoriously open about allowing readers to interpret his work, declaring: "The poet is entitled to everything the reader can find in the poem." There are no "right" or "wrong" answers here.

Other prospective members can be reached through a note on community bulletin boards (in the library or supermarket) or an announcement in the local newspaper or radio station. Since the group should be small, a large response is not needed.

Get together.

Find a suitable time and a place to meet. Rooms can often be reserved in the public library, a neighborhood school, or a religious center. Or you can invite the group to meet in your home initially.

To get the first discussion started all you need is a copy of the poem. (This book is a good place to begin.) To give everyone a taste of what they will be doing, a well-known poem such as "The Road Not

Taken" is a good icebreaker. As with every poem, it should first be read aloud, one verse per person. Then each reader will tell what the poem has meant to her or him. Anyone who chooses to may pass. Individuals can comment on any specific word, or line, or passage that impressed them or can ask questions about aspects they did not understand. (The narrative-commentary accompanying each poem in this book may provide some answers.)

The variety of interpretations is invariably amazing, and sometimes what one person finds in the poem will be in total disagreement with what another sees in it. This happens often in interpreting poetry, but is especially true of the responses to Frost's poems. He delights in sending contradictory signals to his readers. He was regularly of two minds about many things—roads, walls, work, nature, society, God, and almost everything else he wrote about. He proposes questions that set us wondering, but he does not give us clear-cut answers. It is in turning the ideas over in our minds that we learn and grow. At the end of the discussion, with some of the possibilities explored, the poem should be read aloud again, allowing each listener to hear in it what he or she chooses.

The rest of the first meeting will be spent on deciding when, where, and how often the group wants to meet. Once a month or every two weeks works well, the choice depending on the members' other commitments. Whatever the group decides, the schedule should be consistent: for example, every third Wednesday of the month from 7:00 to 9:00 or every other Thursday afternoon from 1:00 to 3:00. Two hours is usually long enough for the group to become immersed in the poetry, but short enough to keep all interested and involved.

The poem or poems for the next session should be chosen. To begin with, they can be individual favorites, two shorter poems per session or one long one. More than three poems per meeting will probably be too many.

A good way to close the first meeting is with a look at the questions given below. This bare-bones list may be used to enrich the group's understanding of a poem. The questions are intended to suggest other ways of getting into it and opening up new avenues to explore. If time permits, to familiarize the group with the questions, the list might be tried out on "The Road Not Taken." Or the group may choose to wait until the second session to apply the questions. All of them do not necessarily have to be used with each poem:

(1) What is the setting of the poem?
(2) What kind of person is the speaker in the poem?
(3) Is the poem addressed to the reader or to someone else?
(4) How well does the basic metaphor of the poem work? (choosing a road is like making a life-decision)
(5) What kind of imagery is used? (things we see, hear, feel).
(6) Are any word choices especially effective?
(7) What is the tone? (serious, comic, nostalgic, reverential, ironic, etc.)
(8) What is the significance of the title?
(9) Is the poem's main purpose to tell a story or to describe something?
(10) Does the poem have a regular beat or a rhyme scheme?

Ideally the end of a poem's discussion will leave the group with the feeling that much more remains to be said about it. Its possibilities are inexhaustible, never reducible to a thought. Keeping in mind what Frost said about writing a poem will help prevent us from destroying the poem as we talk about it. In a letter to his friend Louis Untermeyer, Frost wrote: "A poem is never a put-up job so to speak. It begins as a lump in the throat, a sense of wrong, a homesickness, a lovesickness. It is never a thought to begin with. It is at its best when it is a tantalizing vagueness." Embrace the vagueness, and give it your own dimensions and reverberations.

Plan ahead.

Once the group has become comfortable with the format, the poems can be chosen thematically. Frost's poetry is rich with repetitive motifs that vary and deepen the individual poems. The list of themes that follow this appendix will unify the poetry yet allow for the contradictions and surprises that are characteristic of Frost's work. Poetry is most fully experienced through rereading. Listing the poems under several classifications encourages discussing each selection from different perspectives, the poem becoming richer with each reading and each point-of-view explored.

For example, the most simple, obvious, and satisfying classification is one based on the seasons. The group can decide to read all the spring poems together, or to cover all four seasons in succession with a representative poem for each, or to combine a spring poem with a fall poem for contrast. The possibilities remain open, and the same is true for all the other listings.

Another option is to read the poems in this book in the order in which they appear and to focus on the three themes that are built into the book: the New England background, Frost's poetic development, and his life story. The poems have been selected because they are about the landscape and people of New England, an area Frost has made uniquely his own. Since the poems are arranged chronologically according to when they were written, reading them in sequence will reveal how Frost developed as a poet and found his distinctive voice and style. The biographical approach is provided in the narrative-commentaries that accompany each poem, where many of the details of his life illuminate the poetry. These three perspectives as well as the thematic groupings that follow should lead readers to new combinations and pairings as well as to the many other poems Robert Frost has written.

Although the success of a Frost poetry circle is in no way dependent on outside research, some readers may choose to read further in the many biographies and critiques Frost's poetry has generated. The bibliography of works cited in this book covers a representative sampling. The internet has several web sites that offer additional reading lists, brief biographies, chronologies, selected poems and commentaries. The most useful are:

http://www.english.uiuc.edu/maps/poets/a_f/frost/frost.htm

http://www.libarts.sfasu.edu/frost/index.html

http://www.poets.org/lit/poet/rfrostst.html

http://www.derry.nh.us/frost.html

http://www.hearts-ease.org/library/frost/index.html

http://www.amherstcommon.com/walking_tour/frost.html

The best internet source for beginning Frost poetry circles, however, is http://www.frostfriends.org.

This Web site is maintained by the Friends of Robert Frost, Inc., whose own Frost discussion group can serve as a role model. The members have been meeting informally every other week since founder Carole Thompson organized the first session in 1997. When they were incorporated in February 2000, one of their major goals became the encouragement of adult discussion clubs. They will provide guidelines and advice, and may be reached through their website or by mail at The Friends of Robert Frost, Inc., P. O. Box 4586, Bennington VT 05201.

Thematic Groupings of Frost's Poetry

Seasons

Spring
A Prayer in Spring
Putting in the Seed
Pea Brush
The Pasture
Mending Wall

Summer
The Tuft of Flowers
Mowing
Ghost House
Rose Pogonias
The Oven Bird
Hyla Brook
The Exposed Nest
An Encounter

Autumn
My Butterfly
Reluctance
Waiting
A Late Walk
October
My November Guest
Going for Water
After Apple-Picking
The Cow in Apple-Time
The Road Not Taken

Winter
Stars
An Old Man's Winter Night
Storm Fear
Good Hours

Winter (cont.)   The Wood-Pile
                       Birches

Being alone

Into My Own
Reluctance
The Vantage Point
Ghost House
An Old Man's Winter Night
Storm Fear
Good Hours
The Sound of the Trees

Being with others

The Tuft of Flowers
Time to Talk
The Pasture
The Wood-Pile
Mending Wall
Birches
The Death of the Hired Man

Making choices

Into My Own
Reluctance
The Vantage Point
The Death of the Hired Man
The Wood-Pile
Birches
The Sound of the Trees
The Exposed Nest
The Road Not Taken

Death/grief/loss

Stars
Home Burial
"Out-Out—"

Faith and despair

Faith
A Prayer in Spring
October
Rose Pogonias

Despair
Stars
Storm Fear
The Wood-Pile

Love

Elinor related
Waiting
A Late Walk
My November Guest
Putting in the Seed
The Pasture

General
Hyla Brook
Birches
The Death of the Hired Man

Fear
An Old Man's Winter Night
Storm Fear
The Wood-Pile
Birches
The Sound of the Trees

Stages of life
Birches
The Road Not Taken
Oven Bird
After Apple-Picking
An Old Man's Winter Night
The Death of the Hired Man

Loyalty to oneself

Into My Own
Reluctance

Nature

Trees

A Prayer in Spring
My November
Pea Brush
Oven Bird
Mending Wall
After Apple-Picking
Birches
The Sound of the Trees
Putting in the Seed

Flowers/Plants

The Tuft of Flowers
A Late Walk
The Vantage Point
Mowing
Ghost House
Rose Pogonias
October
Putting in the Seed
A Prayer in Spring
Pea Brush
Hyla Brook
The Wood-Pile
An Encounter

Living Creatures

My Butterfly
Waiting
The Tuft of Flowers
A Late Walk
Vantage Point
Mowing
Ghost House
October

Creatures (cont.)	A Prayer in Spring
	Pea Brush
	The Oven Bird
	Hyla Brook
	The Pasture
	After Apple-Picking
	The Cow in Apple-Time
	The Exposed Nest

Walking

Reluctance
A Late Walk
Good Hours
The Wood-Pile
The Road Not Taken

Joking poems

The Cow in Apple-Time
The Road Not Taken
October
An Encounter

Poems showing influence of other writers

Into My Own
Waiting
Rose Pogonias
The Oven Bird
Hyla Brook
Home Burial
"Out, Out—"
Ghost House
October
The Wood-Pile
After Apple-Picking
The Road Not Taken

Poems about poetry

The Tuft of Flowers
October
The Oven Bird
Mowing

Notable sound imagery

After Apple-Picking
Birches
Ghost House
Going for Water
The Oven Bird
An Old Man's Winter Night

Good examples of "talk-song"

Mowing
My November Guest
A Time to Talk
Birches
Home Burial
The Death of the Hired Man

Alphabetical Listing
of Poems

After Apple-Picking 72

Birches 76

Cow in Apple Time, The 86

Death of the Hired Man, The 42

Encounter, An 100

Exposed Nest, The 90

Ghost House 24

Going for Water 40

Good Hours.. 62

Home Burial 80

Hyla Brook 56

Into My Own 6

Late Walk, A 16

Mending Wall 68

Mowing 22

My Butterfly 2

My November Guest 34

October 30

Old Man's Winter Night, An 54

"Out, Out—" 96

Oven Bird, The 52

Pasture, The.. 58

Pea Brush 50

Prayer in Spring, A 32

Putting in the Seed 38

Reluctance 8
Road Not Taken, The 94
Rose Pogonias 28
Sound of the Trees, The 88
Stars 18
Storm Fear 60
Time to Talk, A 36
Tuft of Flowers, The 12
Vantage Point, The 20
Waiting 10
Wood-Pile, The 64

Backnotes for Sources
by Paragraphs

Introduction (*xiii - xv*)

1: "I want to . . .": Thompson *Early* 438.

5: "I have written . . .": c. April 19, 1932, letter to Sidney Cox, Thompson *Letters* 385; "You must not . . .": July 10, 1913, letter to Sidney Cox, Evans 26; "Every poem of . . .": Evans 90.

6: "autobiographical": Mertins 72.

9: "literature begins with . . .": Cook *Dimensions* 7; "There ought to . . .": 1958 talk at Bread Loaf, Poirier ix; "I talk about . . .": Cook *Voice* 23; 20,000 copies: Stetson 23.

10: "All the fun's . . .": "The Mountain" in *North of Boston*.

My Butterfly (2 -3)

1: wrote My Butterfly at eighteen: Untermeyer 61.

2: dropping out of Dartmouth, teaching in Salem, NH, living in Lawrence with mother and sister: Thompson *Early* 145-46, 162-64.

3: writing 'My Butterfly': Thompson *Early* 518-19; "It was like . . .": Sergeant 34; "first real poem": Angyal, 111.

4: "get the stuff . . .": Barry 141.

5: printed in "Twilight": Thompson *Early* 174.

6: "When I first . . .," "The young poet . . .": Mertins 197-98.

7: "for sentiment, perhaps": Mertins 197.

Into My Own (6 - 7)

1: "to feel really . . .": Newdick 43-44; completed in 1901: Angyal 98.

2: "went away from . . .": February 26, 1913, letter to John Bartlett in Anderson 37; leaving Dartmouth: Thompson *Early* 145-46; Dismal Swamp episode: Thompson *Early* 173-89.

3: "Love alters not with his brief hours and weeks, / But bears it out even to the edge of doom" from Shakespeare's sonnet 116: Cramer 14.

4: adolescent bravado: Haymes 454-55 and Miller 352; stubborn resistance to change: Parini 119 and Brower 230; "really about loyalty": Ciardi "American Bard" 54; "Emersonian idea": Cook *Voice* 190; "That, again, is . . .": Cook *Voice* 189-190.

5: "desire for the . . .": Cook *Voice* 189; "longing for the . . .": MacLeish 443.

Reluctance (8)

1: Frost's call on Elinor at St. Lawrence in Canton: Thompson *Early* 173-76.

2: Frost's jealousy, the Dismal Swamp episode, Elinor's denials: Thompson *Early* 168-71, 176-188, 169.

3: written in late fall 1894: Newdick 164, Thompson *Early* 188-89; "Even a season . . .": Lathem and Thompson *Poetry* 410-11.

4: "morbid now" letter dated December 4, 1894, to Susan Hayes Ward: Thompson *Letters* 24-25; "written a great . . .": Lathem and Thompson *Poetry* 410-11.

Waiting (10)

1: too "personal": Amherst College, Robert Frost Memorial Library, MS 219 cited in Cramer 19; written before 1895 in Lawrence: Angyal 103; or in Salem: Angyal 108; living in Lawrence and Salem between 1892 and 1895: Thompson *Early* 147-213.

2: odd jobs: Thompson *Early* 147-213.

3: "gentle": Amherst College, Robert Frost Memorial Library, MS 219, Cramer 19.

4: "all the best . . .": preface to *Palgrave's Treasury* xvii; bought at Dartmouth, read to his children, assigned to his students: Thompson *Early* 142, 307, 347.

5: less turbulent relationship in spring 1895: Thompson *Early* 201-203; wedding, "ominous elements" for future: Thompson *Early* 211-213.

The Tuft of Flowers (12 - 13)

1: working on Dinsmore farm in 1891: Thompson *Early* 103; "mowed by hand . . .": Cook *Voice* 85.

2: "one of the earliest . . .": Cook *Voice* 113; Harvard composition class in 1897: Thompson *Early* 235.

3: "little Tommy Tucker . . .," "too timid to . . .": February 26, 1913, letter to John Bartlett, Anderson 37; "it made a hit . . .": Mertins 90; Pinkerton Academy teaching position: Thompson *Early* 321; published in Derry paper: Cramer 23.

4: "togetherness": Cook *Voice* 84; Anderson 37; "I was thinking . . .": Cook *Voice* 113; "away from people . . .": Anderson 37.

5: "same subject . . .": Robbins 5; "the social part . . .": Cook *Voice* 189; because he liked them: Cook *Voice* 180; not for self-conscious reasons: Cook *Voice* 85; "The heart of . . .": Mertins 78; "That's where the poetry . . .": Cook *Voice* 113.

6: definition of poetry: Cook *Voice* 189; "exhibitionism," "against the idea . . .": Pritchard *Life* 25.

7: "A poem is . . .": Untermeyer 22; "begins in delight . . .," "must be a . . .": Hyde Cox 17; "I always considered . . .": Mertins 90.

A Late Walk (16)

1: written in 1897: Angyal 98; move from California in 1885: Thompson *Early* 44-46.

2: Loren Bailey's farm, John Dinsmore's farm: Thompson *Early* 86-87, 103; Carl Burell and the honeymoon cottage: Thompson *Early* 217.

3: written as love poem for Elinor: Thompson *Early* 360; Frost and Elinor in summer of 1896: Thompson *Early* 219; "Flower Gathering" written in 1896 in Allenstown: Angyal 108.

Stars (18)

1: begun in Lawrence in 1898 or 1899: Angyal 107; completed in Methuen in 1900: Thompson *Early* 546-47; "It's too late . . .": Thompson *Early* 257-58.

2: Elinor's depression, atheism: Thompson *Early* 258-59; Minerva as goddess of wisdom: Cramer 16.

The Vantage Point (20)

3: original title as "Choice of Society": Sergeant *Trial* 60; written in 1900: Angyal 99; move from Methuen to Derry farm: Thompson *Early* 260-264; "I was a poor . . .": audiotape of 1954 Bread Loaf talk, Middlebury College Library Collection, Parini 75.

4: "The only thing . . .," "turned out right . . .": March 4, 1952, letter to Robert Chase, Thompson *Letters* 552.

Mowing (22 - 23)

1: learns haying from Bailey: Thompson *Early* 86-87.

2: written in 1900: Angyal 99, 108; move to Derry, writing poetry at night: Thompson *Early* 274-275.

3: "one line," "philosophy of art": Cook *Voice* 133; "definition of poetry": Cook *Voice* 189; "Doting on things . . .": Cook *Voice* 133: "a lot to do": Cook *Voice* 123; "In mowing, for . . .": July 17, 1913, letter to Thomas B. Mosher, Thompson *Letters* 83.

4: "talk song": Sergeant *Fire* 295; best poem in his first book: December 1914 letter to Sydney Cox, Evans 56; "Yes, now that's . . .": C. Day Lewis and Robert Frost, "It Takes a Hero to Make a Poem: A Conversation Broadcast, 13th of September, 1957" (*Claremont Quarterly*, vol. 5, no. 3, p. 27) quoted in Cramer 22.

Ghost House (24 - 25)

1: "a time when . . .": audiotape of 1957 talk at Bread Loaf, Amherst College Library Collection, Parini 91; written in 1901: Angyal 98.

2: adjacent to the Derry farm: Thompson *Early* 300; location of cellar hole: Lesley Frost, Notes I, 19, 4-5.

3: burned in 1867, belonged to Merriam: Lesley Frost, Notes, I, 19, 4-5; tall chimney: Thompson *Early* 300.

5: "a poem is . . .": "The Prerequisites," Hyde Cox 97; "I did read . . ." : July 11, 1917, letter to Lewis N. Chase, Barry 75.

6: "sweetly sorrowful": Brower 228; "moving and nonsentimental . . . Yankee condition": Cook *Voice* 18, 19.

7: "into a distant . . .an elusive ideal": Marcus 23-24.

Rose Pogonias (28 - 29)

1: journal entry, neighbor's property (belonged to Mrs. Sarah J. Upton): Lesley Frost, Notes I, 54, 16-17; Notes I, 54, 1; written on Derry farm in 1901: Angyal 99, 108; Carl Burell on Derry farm: Thompson *Early* 263-278; introduced to wild flowers in 1896: Thompson *Early* 217.

2: echoes of Spenser: Poirier 209; of Marvel: Poirier 207; of Wordsworth: Brower 6, 153; of Thoreau: Burnshaw 298, Poirier 207; "language of gems and flowers": Kilcup 157.

3: "I don't see . . .": July 11, 1917, letter to Lewis N. Chase, Barry 75; "Now the manner . . .": "Introduction," *The Arts Anthology* (1925) , Barry 116; "When I first . . .," "It is only . . .": Mertins 197.

October (30 - 31)

2: possibly written in 1901: Angyal 99; written on Derry farm: Thompson *Early* 570, Angyal 108; Nathaniel Head's grapes and retaining wall: Lesley Frost, Notes I, 36, 2-3.

3: influence of reading Yeats, "highly distinct and . . .": Parini 108, 121; original title of "Determined": Pritchard *Life* 65; "humor" balancing sadness: Thompson *Early* 570.

4: "If you want . . .": Cook *Voice* 124; a place "apart . . .contentions," "innocent of everything . . .": Burnshaw 188.

A Prayer in Spring (32 - 33)

2: "Forgive, O Lord . . .": Burnshaw 119; I'm never so serious . . .": recorded by Reginald Cook, cited in Stetson 23; his Presbyterian-Unitarian-Swedenborgian mother: Thompson *Early* 499; not a follower or an enemy but a rethinker: Thompson *Early* 118-20; "I discovered that . . .": October 27, 1917, letter to Louis Untermeyer, Thompson *Letters* 220.

3: Frost's mother's cancer, Elliott's death, diagnosis of tuberculosis, positive response to spring on Derry farm, writing spring poems: Thompson *Early* 253, 259-60; 257-58; 259; 289; xvii.

My November Guest (34 - 35)

1: "a pleasant reminder . . .": Lathem *Robert Frost 100*, 11; written in 1903: Angyal 98; "We had plenty . . .": Mertins 87.

2: earliest attempt to write a "talk song": Sergeant *Fire* 295; "Take My November . . .," "definite entities . . .," "often says more . . .": Anderson 83, 82, 85.

3: "sorrow runs through . . .": Grade 209-10; "the unspoken half . . .": October 4, 1937, letter to Louis Untermeyer, Thompson *Letters* 450.

4: "a new force . . .": March 4, 1912, letter to Thomas B. Mosher, Thompson *Letters* 47.

A Time to Talk (36 - 37)

1: "I didn't know . . .," "talking poems": Mertins 19.

2: "the sound of sense": July 4, 1913, letter to John Bartlett, Anderson 54; wrote the poem in 1905: Angyal 100; "the abstract vitality . . .": Anderson 53; "the odd arrest . . .": Brower 10; counts on readers having heard "What is it?": Brower 9.

4: stone wall on Derry property: Lesley Frost, Notes I, 38-39; II 2, 3-4; John Hall as fellow poultry farmer, Thompson *Early* 282; Frost's fascination with Hall's way of speaking, "perfecting the art . . .": Thompson *Early* 371.

5: chicken farming stories in poultry journals: Lathem and Thompson, *Poultryman* 15; "A Time to Talk" published in *The Prospect* publication of Plymouth Normal, Plymouth NH, in June 1916, collected in *Mountain Interval* in December 1916: Cramer 53.

6: "brilliant, provocative, learned . . .": Stanlis 323.

Putting in the Seed (38)

2: written in 1905: Angyal 100; life during the first five years on the Derry farm: Thompson *Early* 269-289; "the most sacred . . .": Thompson *Triumph* 507.

4: "one of Frost's . . .": Meyers 139; "Yes, I suppose . . .": Thompson *Triumph* 230, 592; "joins creatively in . . .": Poirier 176.

Going for Water (40)

1: "I never invent . . .": Mertins 72; life on the Derry farm: Thompson *Early* 269-312; "five free years," "The only thing . . .": March 4, 1952, letter to Robert Chase, Thompson *Letters* 552.

2: "All poetry to . . .": Thompson *Triumph* 68; "ear for silences": Anderson 71.

3: "hearing imagination rather . . .": July 27, 1914, letter to John Cournos, Thompson *Letters* 130; confluence of feminine and masculine configurations: Miller 363.

The Death of the Hired Man (42 - 43)

2: written in 1905: Newdick 61, Angyal 99; "an idyllic atmosphere . . .": Thompson *Triumph* 50; teaching at Pinkerton: Thompson *Early* 313-323; "time-rich" days on the Derry farm: audiotape of 1954 talk at Bread Loaf, Middlebury College Library collection, Parini 75.

3: "I always wanted . . .": Cook *Voice* 144; haying in his teens: Thompson *Early* 86-87, 103; Carl Burell and his grandfather on Derry farm: Thompson *Early* 263-278.

4: "a little drama . . .": Evans 89.

5: "the way in which . . .": Evans 89; "I like to think . . .": Cook *Voice* 223.

6: Frost's angry response to staged performance: Thompson *Triumph* 60; "the danger is . . .": Thompson *Triumph* 534.

7: "opposing goods" in "To a Young Wretch": Cook *Voice* 282; "the feminine way . . .": Barry 45.

8: "masterpieces of deep . . .": unsigned review by Edward Thomas in August 1914 *English Review*, Pritchard *Life* 89; "got something he . . .": Gould 124.

Pea Brush (50)

1: "all life is . . .": Thompson *Triumph* 68.

2: begun in Derry in 1905: Angyal 100; "I wrote more . . .": March 4, 1952, letter to Robert Chase, Thompson *Letters* 552.

3: "Pea-sticks" in *The Bouquet*: Thompson *Early* 601, Thompson *Triumph* 560.

4: inscription to Lawrance Thompson: Cramer 52.

5: transplanting trillium: Thompson *Early* 300; "the land is . . .": Cook *Voices* 20.

The Oven Bird (52 - 53)

1: "aberrant species": Peterson, 247; orioles and thrushes not singing in mid-summer: Brower 30; oven bird's color, habits, and song: Peterson 246.

2: written in 1906-1907: Thompson *Triumph* 541 (other possible dates of composition 1902 and 1905: Angyal 100, 117); oven-shaped nest: Marcus 71; echo of Dante's *Inferno*: Cramer 50.

3: "make" a poem: Van Doren 75-77; acceptance: Pritchard "Diminished Nature" 475-79; need to persist: Meyers 138; "Dear Oven Bird" in November 16, 1916, letter from Sidney Cox: Evans 130-31; one of Frost's parables: Cook *Voice* 258; "sentence sounds . . .fresh from talk" in February 11, 1914, letter to John Bartlett: Anderson 83; "sing-song": Anderson 84.

An Old Man's Winter Night (54)

3: written in 1906-07 in Derry, Lambert story: Thompson *Triumph* 540.

4: fear of the dark, sleeping in his mother's room: Thompson *Early* 205; summer cottage on Ossipee Mountain: Thompson *Early* 203-04; best poem in *Mountain Interval*: c. December 7, 1916, letter to Sidney Cox, Evans 132, Sergeant *Trial* 179.

Hyla Brook (56)

1: "peepers": Brower 82; exact year uncertain: 1904 in Angyal 100; 1912 in Angyal 117; most probably in 1906 or 1907: Thompson *Triumph* 541; "a little poem . . .": April 25, 1915, letter to John W. Haines: Thompson *Letters* 171.

2: Darwin's book as source for name: Faggen 280; "most exquisite line . . .": Brower 82.

3: Alfred Lord Tennyson, *The Poetical Works of Tennyson*, ed. W. J. Rolfe (Boston: Houghton Mifflin, 1974), 218, 220 as cited in Cramer 49.

4: "clinches the metaphor . . .": Cook *Voice* 55; "Poetry is simply . . .," "saying one thing . . .": Robert Frost "Constant."

The Pasture (58 - 59)

1: "two small pastures": Cramer 10; 1905 walk to the pasture spring: Lesley Frost, Notes I, 37; "I never had . . .": Smythe 56.

2: "a poem about . . .": E. A. Richards, "Two Memoirs of Frost" (*Touchstone*, March 1945, p. 20) quoted in Cramer 10; tempestuous relationship: Thompson *Early* 173-89, 310-12; Katz 15-25, 48-50.

3: Lesley's dream-like incident: Thompson *Early* 308; Carol's denial: Parini 90.

5: "to express the . . .," "the uncloudiness displace . . .": Smythe 56-57; "unclouded": Smythe 56.

Storm Fear (60 - 61)

2: time and place in the poem: Thompson *Early* 279-80; written in Plymouth in 1911: Angyl 98.

3: "Last night there . . .": Lesley Frost, Notes V, 30-31.

4: "I write this . . .,"; "It snowed hard . . .": Grade 75, 79.

5: to give the book coherence: Angyal 104; "You can never . . .": Mertins 107.

6: "I find I . . .": April 27, 1920, letter to G. R. Elliott, Thompson *Letters* 248; a "tighter" poem: Angyal 112; "suppleness of movement," "never quite coming . . .," "only two words . . .": Pritchard *Life* 19.

Good Hours (62 - 63)

1: " a little stanza . . .": Cook *Voices* 112-13; written in Plymouth in winter of 1911-12: Thompson *Early* 433, Angyal 99, 104.

2: his year in Plymouth: Thompson *Early* 369-91; "I must either . . .": Thompson *Triumph* 67.

3: "a master of . . .," "carries a slyly . . .": Cook *Voices* 233.

4: "book of people": dedication of *North of Boston* reads: "To / E. M. F. / THIS BOOK OF PEOPLE."

The Wood-Pile (64 - 65)

1: used as his Christmas card: Burnshaw 164.

2: "largely written" before England: Sergeant *Trial* 119; begun in Derry: Angyal 113, Sergeant 119; "As a bird . . .": Walsh 221.

3: originated in Hawthorne's notebook: Crowley 300.

4: clematis as vine of buttercup family: Cramer 43.

5: "chopping with an ax" and "writing with a pen": Reeve 95.

6: sold Derry farm, move to England: Thompson *Early* 367, 390-91.

7: "parable" poem, "There are intimations . . .": Cook *Voice* 55; division between humanity and nature: Lynen 145, Potter 149, Poirier 143, Squires 73, Crowley 299.

8: two questions: July 11, 1917, letter to Lewis N. Chase, Barry 74; bird passage as displacement: Poirier 141-42.

9: "one of my . . .": Burnshaw 164; "Poetry burns up . . .": anonymous review in July 2, 1914, *London Times Literary Supplement*, p. 316 in Thompson *Early* 451, 601.

Mending Wall (68 - 69)

1: "I wrote the . . .": Thompson *Early* 432-33, 594.

2: trip to Scotland: Francis 89-91, 94-97, 199; "the best," "was the time . . .," "dry stone dykes": c. September 15, 1913, letter to Sidney Cox, Thompson *Letters* 94; stone dykes of Kingsbarns as impetus for "Mending Wall": Walsh 137-43.

3: wall along Guay's property line, Mr. Guay's pine woods: Lesley Frost, Notes I 38-39; II 2, 3-4; Guay helping out the Frosts: Thompson *Early* 285, 313, 339.

4: proverbial phrase in *Blum's Farmer's and Planter's Almanac* (Winston-Salem, NC, p. 13): Cramer 31; "On the way . . .": Lesley Frost, Notes IV 21, 1-11.

5: "Fairies live in . . .," "Their backs were . . .": Robert Frost *Stories* 35, 39.

6: "Maybe I was . . .," "no rigid separation . . .,": Lathem *Interviews* 257, 112; "played exactly fair . . .": Cook "Asides" 355; "I am both . . .", audiotape by Charles Foster of 1938 talk at Breadloaf, Dartmouth College Library Collection, Parini 139.

7: "No, we always . . .": Mertins 353.

8: Frost reading "Mending Wall" in Russia, Frost's meeting with Khrushchev: Thompson and Winnick 316, 318-323; "on both sides . . .": October 1962 letter from August Heckscher, Special Consultant on the Arts, Thompson and Winnick 326, 437.

After Apple-Picking (72 - 73)

1: "one of the great . . .": Kemp 127; "Imagery and after-imagery . . .": Angyal 111.

2: written in Beaconsfield in fall of 1913: Parini 140; "the Magoon place," Carl Burell's help and departure, need for a teaching job: Thompson *Early* 261; 263-64, 277-78; 313-24.

3: "the intoxication of . . .": Evans 90; "observing," "I am too . . .": Cook *Voice* 126-27.

4: Frost's debt to Emerson: Cramer 39; dreamless sleep of animals: Poirier 299; longer sleep of hibernation and hint of death and resurrection: Marcus 52-53.

5: "amused confusion," "incantatory repetitions . . .," "the most beautiful . . .": Brower 26, 24, 23; "freedom perfectly controlled": Brower 23.

6: "dream vision," "very great poems": Poirier 293, 292.

Birches (76 - 77)

1: Charley Peabody teaching timid Rob how to swing birches: Thompson *Early* 59-60; "papa likes to swing": Lesley Frost, Notes II 6.

2: called "Swinging Birches": August 7, 1913, letter to John Bartlett, Thompson *Letters* 89; written in 1913: Walsh 248; "with one stroke . . .": Sergeant *Andes* 300; "'Birches' is two . . .": Brooks 471; earlier draft in 1906: Angyal 100; about icicles: Parini 135.

3: Ipswich story, "birches, straight up . . .": Smythe 55-56; "she wouldn't come . . .": Smythe 56; "It was almost . . .": audiotape Amherst College Library Collection, Parini 22.

4: "a hi birch . . .," "At first I . . .": Lesley Frost, Notes II 2; II 5; "there are no . . .": Lentricchia 101.

5: "It isn't in . . .": Anderson 175; "striving to get . . .," "I should expect . . .": "Poverty and Rural Life: An Interview with Robert Frost" (*Rural America*, June 1931, p. 5) quoted in Cramer 52; the line that came to mean the most: Cook 51.

6: grove of white paper birches: Untermeyer 194; Wade Van Dore's account of walks "to see the birches," Frost's calling them "lady trees" and talking about "keeping faith" with them: Beck 48.

Home Burial (80 - 81)

1: written in Beaconsfield in 1912-1913, Elliott's death, Frost's denial: Thompson *Early* 597, 258, 597.

2: inspired by separation of Leona and Nathaniel Harvey after death of their child, Frost at Ossippie, Harveys' subsequent children: Thompson *Early* 597, 203, 572.

3: "And I suppose . . .": Untermeyer 103; "I refused to . . .": Thompson *Early* 511; "more practical and . . .": Ciardi "Master" 20; Elinor's use of "the world's evil": Thompson *Early* 597; "Some of the . . .": Mertins 72.

4: "too sad": Thompson *Early* 598; "sufficiently self-expressive": July 27, 1914, letter to John Cournos, Thompson *Letters* 130; his use of "oh": Lathem *Interviews* 13; "the four 'dont's' . . .": Evans 89; "gained something from . . .": Thompson *Letters* 130; "that cry of . . .": Lowell 117-18.

5: New England Eclogues as possible title: Thompson *Early* 433; "dropped to an . . .": July 17, 1913, letter to Thomas B. Mosher, Thompson *Letters* 83; "from a printed . . .": Cox 109.

6: speech rhythms overriding meter as tension mounts: Potter 158.

7: battle between the sexes: Swennes 323-34 and Sasso 95-107; "the heart of womanhood": William Dean Howells, "Editor's Easy Chair" (Harper's, September 1918, p. 635) quoted in Thompson *Triumph* 57; also Frost's "insight into the lives of women": Rittenhouse 247; "miscommunication": Parini 70.

The Cow in Apple Time (86)

1: "my innate mischievousness": November 1, 1927, letter to Leonidas W. Payne, Jr., Thompson *Letters* 344; written in England in 1914: Angyal 100; run-away cow on Derry farm: Lesley Frost, Notes I, 14; I, 49; I, 21; III, 1; III, 8-9; hill on adjoining Guay property: Lesley Frost, Notes V 41.

2: "the giant animals . . .": Cook *Voice* 113; living in rented room in London April, May 1914: Francis 200; "heroic-sized": Cook "Asides" 356.

3: "cruder": Cook, *Voice* 113; "frankly humorous": Untermeyer 207; "delightful": Newdick 91; "delicious": Gould 168; "some have read . . ." Untermeyer 207; "a puritanical farm . . .": Thompson *Early* 605.

The Sound of the Trees (88 - 89)

1: "I never saw . . .": March 22, 1915, letter to William Stanley Baithwaite, Thompson *Letters* 160; written in Dymock: Mertins 128; shared cottage with Abercrombies: Thompson *Triumph* 37;

under influence of Lascelles Abercrombie: October 22, 1917, letter to Amy Lowell, Thompson *Letters* 220; thinking of a group of trees near his old home in New England: Mertins 128.

2: "Do you find . . ..": July 11, 1917, letter to Lewis N. Chase, Barry 74; "The Sound of Trees": Frost eliminated the second "the" in the title when the poem appeared in his *Collected Poems*.

3: desire to set out for the unknown: Parini 49.

4: deliberate foil to "The Road Not Taken": McPhillips 98.

The Exposed Nest (90 - 91)

1: written in 1915 in Franconia, NH: Thompson *Triumph* 541; recalls writing it in 1913 and showing it to his friend Edward Thomas in England: Angyal 100, 114; incident occurred on Derry farm: Thompson *Triumph* 541.

3: "can be beautifully . . .," "a less subtle . . .," "We might observe . . .," "unwillingness to exploit . . .": Pritchard *Life* 152-53.

4: influence of Josiah Royce's lectures at Harvard: Parini 63.

The Road Not Taken (94 - 95)

1: Americans' favorite poem: Hartman, April 4, 2000.

2: friendship with Thomas: Thompson *Early* 441, 452-467; *Triumph* 87-88; "No matter which . . .": Thompson *Triumph* 88.

3: "while I was . . ..": Thompson *Triumph* 546; written in 1914 in England and in 1915 in New Hampshire: Angyal 99, 77; Thomas as target: Thompson *Letters* xv.

4: archetypal symbol of crossroads: see Cramer 45-46 for forerunners such as Virgil, Longfellow, Dickinson, Emerson, and Thoreau; "Two lonely cross-roads . . .": February 10, 1912, letter to Susan Hayes Ward, Sergeant *Trial* 87.

5: "be careful . . .": Cook *Voice* 12; "You can go . . .," "that talks past . . .," took it as a compliment: Cook *Voice* 123.

"Out, Out—" (96 - 97)

1: "too cruel to . . .": Meyers 139; Frost's relationship with Raymond Fitzgerald: Thompson *Early* 342-43, 567; Frost's knowledge of the accident through the Lynches: Thompson *Early* 364, 566-67.

2: written in New Hampshire after return from England: Thompson *Triumph* 541; in summer of 1915: Parini 167; view from Frost's farm near Sugar Hill: Parini 163; view from Fitzgerald's farm: Thompson *Early* 342.

3: *Littleton Courier* story, "Raymond Tracy Fitzgerald . . .": Thompson *Early* 567.

5: "that perfectly organized . . .," "in a flash . . . .": Lynen 31-35.

6: Elliott's death: Thompson *Early* 258; "uncomfortable": Evans 113; cold and stern: Squires 47; "sincere": Evans 113; "natural": Marcus 80; economically necessary: Parini 70; "deadly directness," "mutually accusing ideas": Squires 47.

7: Shakespeare's Macbeth, V. v. 23-28.

8: Herman Melville's "Hawthorne and his Mosses"; account of Trilling's speech: Burnshaw 104-105.

An Encounter (100)

1: written in 1916: Angyal 100; in Vermont near Lake Willoughby: Robert Frost Memorial Library Archives at Amherst College 16 (1916) c4, 47 cited in Cramer 53; camping the summer of 1909: Thompson *Early* 350-54.

2: anti-progress leanings: Parini 298; "even for the least . . .": Thompson *Triumph* 601; "Electricity has come . . ." August 22, 1935, letter, Grade 182.

3: "Whatever progress may . . .": Thompson *Triumph* 387; "bog trotting" as religious experience: Thompson *Early* 223.

4: Frost championing the idea of uselessness: Squires 74; Calypso Bulbosa as virtually extinct: Cramer 54; never more serious than when he's fooling: Reginald Cook in Stetson 23.

How to Start a Frost Poetry Circle (104 - 108)

3: "The poet is . . .": Cook *Voice* 240.

9: "A poem is . . .": Untermeyer 22.

Bibliography of Works Cited

Anderson, Margaret Bartlett. *Robert Frost and John Bartlett: The Record of a Friendship*. New York: Holt, Rinehart, and Winston, 1963.

Angyal, Andrew J. "Robert Frost's Poetry Before 1913, A Checklist." *Proof 5, The Yearbook of American Bibliographical and Textual Studies*. Columbia, SC: J. Faust, 1977.

Barry, Elaine. *Robert Frost on Writing*. New Brunswick, NJ: Rutgers University Press, 1973.

Beck, Jane C. *The Gulley: A Place Apart*. Montpelier VT: Norman and Frances Lear, 1984.

Brooks, Cleanth, and Robert Penn Warren. *Understanding Poetry*. New York: Holt, Rinehart and Winston, 1976.

Brower, Reuben. *The Poetry of Robert Frost: Constellations of Intention*. New York: Oxford University Press, 1963.

Burnshaw, Stanley. *Robert Frost Himself*. New York: G. Braziller, 1986.

Ciardi, John. "Robert Frost: American Bard." *Saturday Review* (24 March 1962): 15-17, 52-54

_____. "Robert Frost: Master Conversationalist at Work." *Saturday Review* (21 March 1959): 17-20, 54.

Cook, Reginald L. *Dimensions of Robert Frost*. New York: Rinehart, 1958.

_____. *Robert Frost: A Living Voice*. Amherst: University of Massachusetts Press, 1974.

_____. "Robert Frost's Asides on his Poetry." *American Literature* 19 (1948): 351-359.

Cox, Hyde and Edward Connery Lathem, eds. *Selected Prose of Robert Frost*. New York: Collier, 1966.

Cox, Sidney. *A Swinger of Birches: A Portrait of Robert Frost.* New York: New York University Press, 1957.

Cramer, Jeffrey S. *Robert Frost Among His Poems: A Literary Companion to the Poet's Own Biographical Contexts and Associations.* Jefferson, NC and London: McFarland, 1996.

Crowley, J. Donald. "Hawthorne and Frost: The Making of a Poem." *Frost Centennial Essays.* Jackson: University Press of Mississippi, 1974. 288-309.

Evans, William R. *Robert Frost and Sidney Cox: Forty Years of Friendship.* Hanover NH: University Press of New England, 1981.

Faggen, Robert. *Robert Frost and the Challenge of Darwin.* Ann Arbor: University of Michigan Press, 1997.

Francis, Lesley Lee. *The Frost Family's Adventures in Poetry: Sheer Morning Gladness at the Brim.* Columbia: University of Missouri Press, 1994.

Frost, Lesley. *New Hampshire's Child: The Derry Journals of Lesley Frost.* Notes and index by Lawrance Thompson and Arnold Grade. Albany: State University of New York Press, 1969.

Frost, Robert. "The Constant Symbol." *Robert Frost: Collected Poems, Prose, and Plays.* Richard Poirier and Mark Richardson, eds. New York: Library of America, 1956. 786-791.

_____. *Stories for Lesley.* Roger D. Sell, ed. Bibliographical Society of the Univ. of Virginia: Univ. Press of Virginia, 1984.

Gould, Jean. *Robert Frost: The Aim Was Song.* New York: Dodd Mead, 1964.

Grade, Arnold, ed. *Family Letters of Robert and Elinor Frost.* Albany: State University of New York Press, 1972.

Hartman, Carl. "Nation Favors 'The Road Not Taken.'" Associated Press release on Netscape, Washington, D.C., April 4, 2000.

Haymes, Donald T. "The Narrative Unity of *A Boy's Will.*" *PMLA* 87 (1972): 452-64.

Katz, Sandra Lee. *Elinor Frost: A Poet's Wife.* Westfield: Institute for Massachusetts Studies, Westfield State College, 1988.

Kemp, John C. *Robert Frost and New England: The Poet as Regionalist.* Princeton NJ: Princeton University Press, 1979.

Kilcup, Karen L. *Robert Frost and Feminine Literary Tradition.* Ann Arbor: University of Michigan Press, 1998.

Lathem, Edward Connery, ed. *Interviews with Robert Frost.* New York: Holt, Rinehart, & Winston, 1966.

_____. *Robert Frost 100.* Boston: David R. Godine, 1974.

_____ and Lawrance Thompson. *Robert Frost: Farm-Poultryman.* Hanover NH: Dartmouth Publications, 1963.

_____. *Robert Frost: Poetry and Prose.* New York: Holt, Rinehart and Winston, 1972.

Lentricchia, Frank. *Robert Frost: Modern Poetics and the Landscape of Self.* Durham NC: Duke University Press, 1975.

Lowell, Amy. *Tendencies in Modern Poetry.* New York: Macmillan, 1917.

Lynen, John F. *The Pastoral Art of Robert Frost.* New Haven: Yale University Press, 1960.

MacLeish, Archibald. "Robert Frost and New England." *National Geographic* 149 (1976): 438-444.

Marcus, Mordecai. *The Poems of Robert Frost: An Explication.* Boston: G. K. Hall, 1991.

McPhillips, Robert T. "Diverging and Converging Paths: Horizontal and Vertical Movement in Robert Frost's *Mountain Interval.*" *American Literature* 58 (1986): 82-98.

Mertins, Louis. *Robert Frost: Life and Talks-Walking.* Norman: University of Oklahoma Press, 1965.

Meyers, Jeffrey. *Robert Frost: A Biography.* New York: Houghton Miflin, 1996.

Miller, Lewis H., Jr. "Design and Drama in A Boy's Will." *Frost Centennial Essays.* Jackson: University Press of Mississippi, 1974. 351-368.

Newdick, Robert. *Newdick's Season of Frost: An Interrupted Biography of Robert Frost.* William A. Sutton, ed. Albany: State University of New York Press, 1976.

Parini, Jay. *Robert Frost: A Life.* New York: Henry Holt, 1999.

Peterson, Roger Tory. *A Field Guide to the Birds.* Boston: Houghton Mifflin, 1980.

Poirier, Richard. *Robert Frost: The Work of Knowing.* New York: Oxford University Press, 1977.

Potter, James L. *Robert Frost Handbook.* University Park: Pennsylvania State University Press, 1980.

Pritchard, William H. "Diminished Nature." *Massachusetts Review* 1(1960):475-92.

_____. *Frost: A Literary Life Reconsidered.* New York: Oxford University Press, 1984.

Reeve, F. D. *Robert Frost in Russia.* Boston: Little, Brown, 1964.

Rittenhouse, Jessie. "Portraits of Women." *Recognition of Robert Frost: Twenty-fifth Anniversary.* Richard Thornton, ed. New York: Henry Holt, 1937.

Robbins, J. Albert. *An Interlude with Robert Frost: Being a Brief Correspondence with the Poet and Recollections.* Bloomington, IN: The Private Press of Frederic Brewer, 1982.

Sasso, Laurence J., "Robert Frost: Love's Question." *New England Quarterly* 42 (1969): 95-107.

Sergeant, Elizabeth Shepley. *Fire Under the Andes: A Group of North American Portraits.* Port Washington NY: Kennikat Press, 1966.

_____. *Robert Frost: The Trial by Existence.* New York: Holt, Rinehart, and Winston, 1960.

Smythe, Daniel. *Robert Frost Speaks.* New York: Twayne, 1964.

Squires, Radcliffe. *The Major Themes of Robert Frost.* Ann Arbor: University of Michigan Press, 1963.

Stanlis, Peter J. "Robert Frost: The Conversationalist as Poet." *Modern Age: A Quarterly Review* (Fall 1997): 323-334.

Stetson, Fred. "The Gully Years." *Vermont Life* (Winter 1992): 18-23.

Swennes, Robert H. "Man and Wife: The Dialogue of Contraries in Robert Frost's Poetry," *American Literature* 42 (1971): 363-72.

Thompson, Lawrance. *Robert Frost: The Early Years, 1874-1915*. New York: Holt, Rinehart, and Winston, 1966.

_____. *Robert Frost: The Years of Triumph, 1915-1938*. New York: Holt, Rinehart and Winston, 1970.

_____, ed. *Selected Letters of Robert Frost*. New York: Holt, Rinehart and Winston, 1964.

_____ and R. H. Winnick. *Robert Frost: The Later Years, 1938-1963*. New York: Holt, Rinehart and Winston, 1976.

Untermeyer, Louis. *Letters of Robert Frost to Louis Untermeyer*. New York: Holt, Rinehart, and Winston, 1963.

Van Doren, Mark. *Introduction to Poetry*. New York: William Sloane, 1951.

Walsh, John Evangelist. *Into My Own: The English Years of Robert Frost, 1912-1915*. New York: Grove Press, 1988.

Index

Abercrombie, Lascelles, 88
After Apple-Picking
    Essay, 72-73
    Poem, 74-75
Allenstown, NH, 16
Anderson, Margaret Bartlett, 117,
    118, 121, 122, 125, 129
Angyal, Andrew J., 117, 118, 119,
    120, 121, 122, 123, 124, 125, 126,
    127, 128, 129
Aristotle, 42

Bailey, Loren, 16, 22
Baithwaite, William Stanley, 126
Barry, Elaine, 117, 120, 122, 124,
    127, 129
Bartlett, John, 34, 77, 118, 121, 122,
    125
Beaconsfield, England, 68, 72, 76, 80
Beck, Jane C., 125, 129
Birches, 88
    Essay, 76-77
    Poem, 78-79
Bouquet, The (RF—Frost children's
    magazine), 50
Boy's Will, A (RF—first collection of
    poetry), 16, 40, 60
Brooks, Cleanth, 125, 129
Brower, Reuben, 36, 73, 117, 120,
    121, 122, 123, 125, 129
Burell, Carl, 16, 28, 42, 60, 72, 100
Burnshaw, Stanley, 120, 124, 128, 129

Calypso Bulbosa, 100, 101, 128
Chase, Lewis N., 120, 124, 127
Chase, Robert, 119, 121, 122
Ciardi, John, 117, 126, 129

Cold War, 69
Cook, Reginald, 25, 43, 52, 62,117,
    118, 119, 120, 122, 123, 124, 125,
    126, 127, 128, 129
Cournos, John, 81, 121, 126
Cow in Apple Time, The
    Essay, 86
    Poem, 87
Cox, Hyde, 118, 120, 129
Cox, Sidney, 30, 73, 81, 117, 122,
    123, 124, 126, 130
Cramer, Jeffrey S., 117, 118, 119, 121,
    122, 123, 124, 125, 127, 128, 130
Crowley, J. Donald, 124, 130

Dante, 97
    Inferno, 52
Dartmouth College, 2, 6, 10
Darwin, Charles (*Voyage of the Beagle*),
    56
Death of the Hired Man, The
    Essay, 42-43
    Poem, 44-49
Derry Enterprise, The, 12, 54
Derry, NH, 20
Derry (NH) chicken farm, 20, 22, 24,
    32, 34, 36, 38, 40, 50, 58, 64-65,
    68-69, 72, 86, 90
Dickinson, Emily, 127
Dinsmore, John, 16
"Directive" (RF—poem), 25
Dismal Swamp (VA), 6
District School Number Nine (S.
    Salem, NH), 6

Elliott, G. R., 123
Emerson, Ralph Waldo, 73, 127

Encounter, An
  Essay, 100-101
  Poem, 101
Evans, William R., 117, 119, 122,
  123, 125, 126, 127, 130
Exposed Nest, The
  Essay, 90-91
  Poem, 92-93

Faggen, Robert, 123, 130
Firth of Fay, 68
Fitzgerald, Michael, 96
Fitzgerald, Raymond, 96
Foster, Charles, 124
Francis, Lesley Lee, 124, 126, 130
Franconia, NH, 90
Frost, Carol (son), 32, 34, 38, 60, 69
Frost, Elinor White (wife), 3, 6, 10,
  16, 18, 20, 33, 34, 40, 58, 60, 80,
  90
Frost, Elliott (son), 18
  death from cholera, 18, 32, 34,
    80, 97
Frost, Irma (daughter), 32, 34, 38
Frost, Isabelle Moodie (mother), 2,
  18, 32
Frost, Jeanie (sister), 2
Frost, Lesley (daughter), 20, 28, 34,
  58, 60, 68, 69, 76, 86, 119, 120,
  121, 123, 124, 125, 126, 130
Frost, Marjorie (daughter), 38
Frost, Robert
  biographical information
    Derry (NH) farm life, 20,
      22, 24, 32, 34, 36, 38,
      40, 50, 58, 64-65, 68-69,
      72, 86, 90
    relationship with Elinor, 6,
      8, 10, 34, 58-59, 80
    haying, 12, 16, 22, 42
    health, 32, 68
    life in England, 65, 68, 72, 95
    religion (belief in God), 18,
      32, 100

Frost, Robert
  biographical information (*cont.*)
    response to death, 80, 97
    teaching, 6, 12, 30, 62, 72
    walking, 2, 6, 16, 52, 59,
      68
    wildflowers/plants, 16, 28,
      50, 94, 100
  commentary on the craft and
    content of poetry, 13, 22, 30-
    31, 36, 40, 56, 72
      everyday speech as poetry
        ("talk song," "the sound
        of sense"), 22-23, 34, 36,
        37, 38, 43, 52-53, 77,
        81, 95
      fact as basis of poetry, 2,
        22, 40, 50, 80-81
      joy in creation, 2, 13
      metaphor, 56
      poetic voice, 3, 29, 34
      sound, matter of, 40
  influences in poetry
    New England landscape/
      setting, 7, 10, 18, 20, 22,
      24, 30, 50, 56, 62, 64
    New England/Yankee
      character, 20, 25, 36, 54
    previous poets, 3, 6, 10,
      24-25, 28-29, 30, 42,
      43, 52, 56, 64, 73, 81,
      88, 97, 116, 120, 123,
      127, 131
  themes/content of poetry
    confusion/clarity, 59
    contradiction/indecision,
      88-89, 94
    humor 30, 62, 94, 100
    isolation/loneliness, 13, 20,
      25, 54, 60, 61, 65, 77
    nature, 10, 20, 52, 56, 61,
      90-91
    prayer, 30, 32

Frost, Robert
   themes/content *(cont.)*
      resistance to change/
        progress, 6, 97, 100
      social interaction, 13, 77
      stoicism/endurance, 52, 54,
        91, 97
      thematic groupings, 109-
        114
      threat in poems, 65, 88
      togetherness, 12, 13, 59, 90
Frost, William Prescott (grandson),
   100
Frost, William Prescott, Jr. (father),
   32

Ghost House
   Essay, 24-25
   Poem, 26-27
Going for Water
   Essay, 40,
   Poem, 41
Good Hours
   Essay, 62-63
   Poem, 63
Gould, Jean, 122, 126, 130
Grade, Arnold, 121, 123, 128, 130
Guay, Napoleon, 24, 68, 86

Haines, John W., 123
Hall, John, 36-37
Hanover, NH, 2
Harvard University, 12, 32, 91
Harvey, Leona (sister-in-law), 80
Harvey, Nathaniel (brother-in-law),
   80
Hawthorne, Nathaniel, 64
   "Young Goodman Brown," 97
Haymes, Donald T., 117, 130
Head, Nathaniel, 30
Heckscher, August, 125
Home Burial, 91
   Essay, 80-81
   Poem, 82-85

Howells, William Dean, 126
Hyde Park, England, 86
Hyla Brook
   Essay, 56
   Poem, 57

In the Clearing (RF—final book of
   poetry), 59
Independent, The, 2
Into My Own
   Poem, 7
   Essay, 6-7

Katz, Sandra Lee, 123, 130
Kemp, John C., 125, 130
Kilcup, Karen L., 120, 131
Krushchev, Nikita, 69

Lake Willoughby (VT), 100
Lambert, Charles, 54
Lankes, J. J., 80
"Last Apple Fall, The" (RF—children's
   story), 69
Late Walk, A
   Essay, 16
   Poem, 17
Lathem, Edward Connery, 118, 121,
   124, 126, 129, 131
Lawrence, MA, 2, 6, 10, 20, 100
Lentricchia, Frank, 125, 131
Lewis, C. Day, 119
Littleton Courier, The, 96
Littleton, NH, 96
London, England, 86
Longfellow, Henry Wadsworth, 127
Lowell, Amy, 81, 126, 127, 131
Lynch, John, 96
Lynch, Margaret, 96
Lynen, John F., 97, 124, 128, 131

MacLeish, Archibald, 7, 117, 131
Marcus, Mordecai, 25, 120, 122, 125,
   127, 131
Marvell, Andrew, 28

McPhillips, Robert T., 88, 127, 131

Melville, Herman, 97

Mending Wall
    Essay, 68-69
    Poem 70-71

Merriam, Charles, 12

Merriam, Marshall, 24

Mertins, Louis, 117, 118, 120, 121,
    123, 125, 126, 127, 131

Methuen, MA, 20

Meyers, Jeffrey, 38, 121, 122, 127, 131

Miller, Lewis H., Jr., 117, 121, 131

Milton, John (*Comus*), 43

Minerva (Roman goddess of wisdom),18

Moscow, Russia, 69

Mosher, Thomas B., 119, 121, 126

Mountain Interval (RF—third
    collection of poetry), 50, 54, 89

Mowing
    Essay, 22-23
    Poem, 23

My Butterfly
    Poem, 4-5
    Essay, 2-3

My November Guest
    Essay, 34-35
    Poem 35

New England Eclogues (title consid-
    ered for *North of Boston*), 81

Newdick, Robert, 117, 118, 122, 126, 131

New York (City), NY, 68

North of Boston (RF—second
    collection of poetry), 58, 62, 64,
    65, 81

October
    Essay, 30-31
    Poem, 31

Old Man's Winter Night, An
    Essay, 54
    Poem, 55

Ossipee Mountain (NH), 54, 80

"Out, Out—", 91
    Essay, 96-97
    Poem, 98-99

Oven Bird, The
    Essay, 52-53
    Poem, 53

Palgrave, Francis (*Golden Treasury*), 10,
    25

Parini, Jay, 30, 88, 117, 119, 120, 122,
    123, 124, 125, 126, 127, 128, 131

Pasture, The
    Essay, 58-59
    Poem, 59

Payne, Leonidas W., Jr., 126

Pea Brush
    Essay, 50
    Poem, 51

Peabody, Charley, 76

Peterson, Roger Tory (*Field Guide to
    the Birds*), 52, 122, 132

Pinkerton Academy, 12, 42

Pinsky, Robert, 94

Plymouth, NH, 30, 60, 62, 94

Plymouth Normal School, 62

Poirier, Richard, 38, 117, 120, 121,
    124, 125, 132

Potter, James L., 124, 126, 132

Prayer in Spring, A
    Essay, 32-33
    Poem 33

Prince Albert Memorial, England, 86

Pritchard, William, 61, 90, 118, 120,
    122, 123, 127, 132

Putting in the Seed
    Essay 38
    Poem 39

Reeve, F. D., 124, 132

Reluctance
    Essay, 8
    Poem, 9

Richards, E. A., 123

Rittenhouse, Jessie, 126, 132

Road Not Taken, The, 88
    Essay, 94-95
    Poem 95
Robbins, J. Allen, 132
Rockwell, Norman, 54
Rolfe, W. J., 123
Rose Pogonias
    Essay, 28-29
    Poem, 29
Royce, Josiah, 91
Ryton, England, 88

Salem Depot, NH, 76
Salem, NH, 2, 10, 16, 22
Sasso, Laurence J., 126, 132
Saturday Evening Post, 54
Selected Poems, 72
Sergeant, Elizabeth Shepley, 117, 119,
    121, 123, 124, 125, 127, 132
Shakespeare, William
    sonnet 116, 6, 117
    Macbeth, 97
Smith, J. C., 68
Smythe, Daniel, 123, 125, 132
Sound of the Trees, The
    Essay, 88-89
    Poem, 89
South Salem, NH, 6
South Shaftsbury, VT, 77
Spenser, Edmund, 28
Squires, Radcliffe, 97, 124, 127, 128,
    132
St. Lawrence University, 10
Stanlis, Peter J., 37, 121, 132
Stars
    Essay, 18
    Poem, 19
"Stopping By Woods on a Snowy
    Evening" (RF—poem), 88
Stetson, Fred, 117, 120, 128, 132
Storm Fear
    Essay, 60-61
    Poem, 61

Sugar Hill, NH, 96
Swennes, Robert H., 126, 132
Tennyson, Alfred Lord, 25, 56, 123
Thomas, Edward, 94, 122
Thompson, Lawrance, 30, 36, 50, 86,
    117, 118, 119, 120, 121, 122, 123,
    124, 125, 126, 127, 128, 133
Thoreau, Henry David, 28, 127
Time to Talk, A
    Essay, 36-37
    Poem 37
Trilling, Lionel, 97
Tuft of Flowers, The
    Essay, 12-13
    Poem, 14-15
"Twilight" (RF—self-published
    collection of poems), 3

Untermeyer, Louis, 13, 80, 86, 117,
    120, 121, 125, 126, 128, 133

Van Doren, Mark, 122, 133
Van Dore, Wade, 125
Vantage Point, The
    Essay, 20
    Poem, 21
Virgil, 81, 127

Waiting
    Essay, 10
    Poem, 11
Walsh, John Evangelist, 124, 125, 133
Ward, Susan Hayes, 118, 127
Warren, Robert Penn, 129
Wilson, Harold, 42
Winnick, R. H., 125
Wood-Pile, The, 25
    Essay, 64-65
    Poem, 66-67
Wordsworth, William, 28

Yeats, William Butler, 25, 30

More Praise for

Robert Frost

The People, Places, and Stories Behind His New England Poetry

"I had a good time strolling and roaming and enjoying the book. The essays are lucidly written and will find an audience, especially among modern New Englanders who may have forgotten how Robert Frost grounded his poetry in their world."

Earl Wilcox, Editor Emeritus, Robert Frost Review

"Focusing on the richest poems in Frost's first three volumes of poetry, this unpretentious but entirely efficient anthology is aimed at the general reader. It warms my heart to see each poem placed skillfully within the context of the poet's everyday existence, conscientious beliefs, and conscious artistry. Its presentation of salient fact welded to sane and suggestive interpretation that is not meant to be exhaustive or exclusionary should give this primer a welcome place in the classroom."

George Monteiro, author of
Robert Frost and the New England Renaissance

"A first-rate intro for everyday readers. The book supplies a graceful, unobtrusive thread of secondary materials and reviews. I think Frost would have been appreciative of Lea Newman's efforts to make his difficult work available to 'all sorts and kinds.'"

Karen Kilcup, author of
Robert Frost and Feminine Literary Tradition